W9-CKX-468

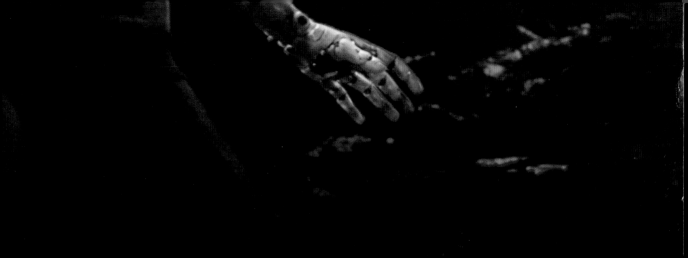

THE ART AND MAKING OF THE MOVIE

Standard edition ISBN: 9781785658082
Limited edition ISBN: 9781785659447

Published by
Titan Books
A division of Titan Publishing Group Ltd
144 Southwark St
London
SE1 0UP

WWW.TITANBOOKS.COM

First edition: December 2018

10 9 8 7 6 5 4 3

™ & © 2018 Twentieth Century Fox Film Corporation.
All rights reserved.

To receive advance information, news, competitions,
and exclusive offers online, please sign up for the
Titan newsletter on our website: www.titanbooks.com

Did you enjoy this book? We love to hear from our readers.
Please e-mail us at: readerfeedback@titanemail.com or
write to Reader Feedback at the above address.

No part of this publication may be reproduced, stored in
a retrieval system, or transmitted, in any form or by any
means without the prior written permission of the publisher,
nor be otherwise circulated in any form of binding or cover
other than that in which it is published and without a similar
condition being imposed on the subsequent purchaser.

A CIP catalogue record for this title is available from the
British Library.

Printed and bound in Italy.

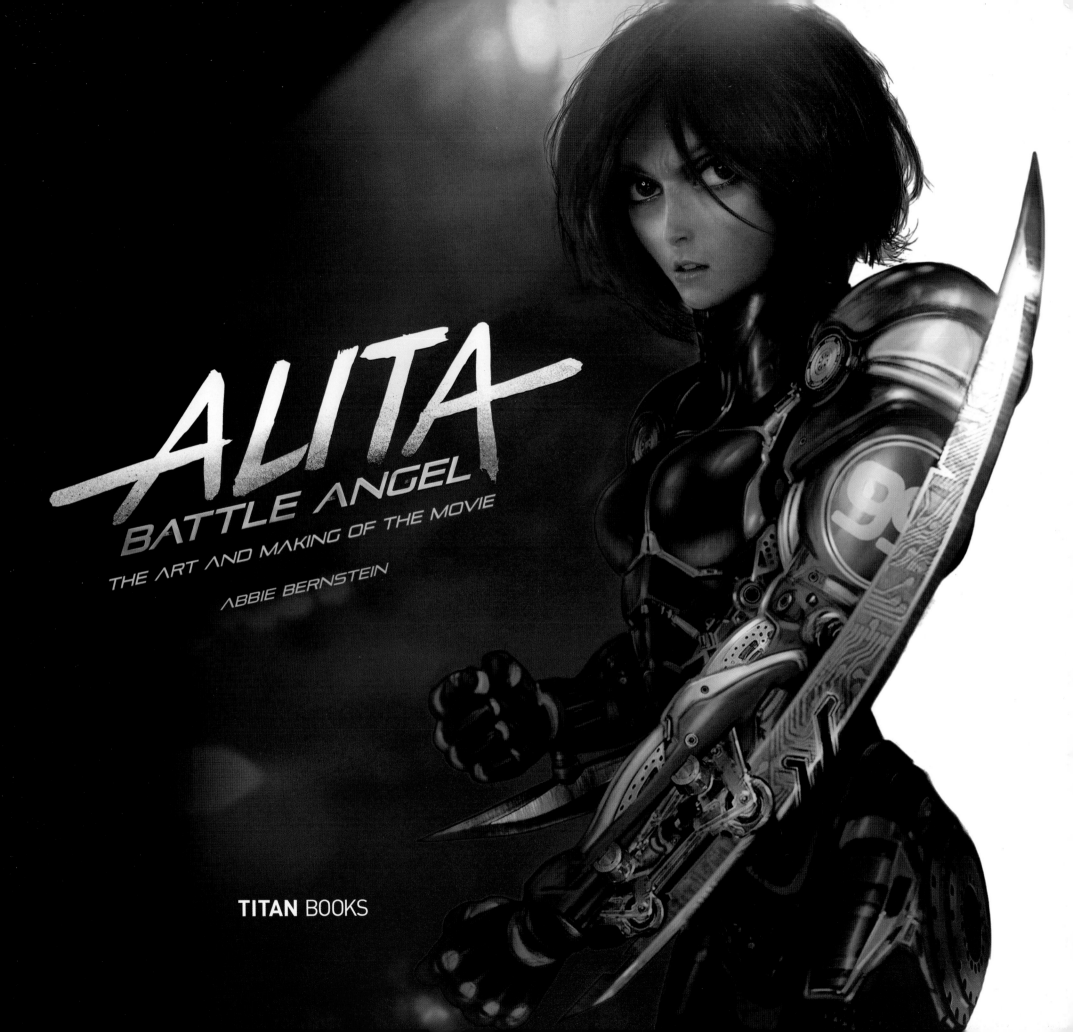

# ALITA
## BATTLE ANGEL
### THE ART AND MAKING OF THE MOVIE

ABBIE BERNSTEIN

**TITAN** BOOKS

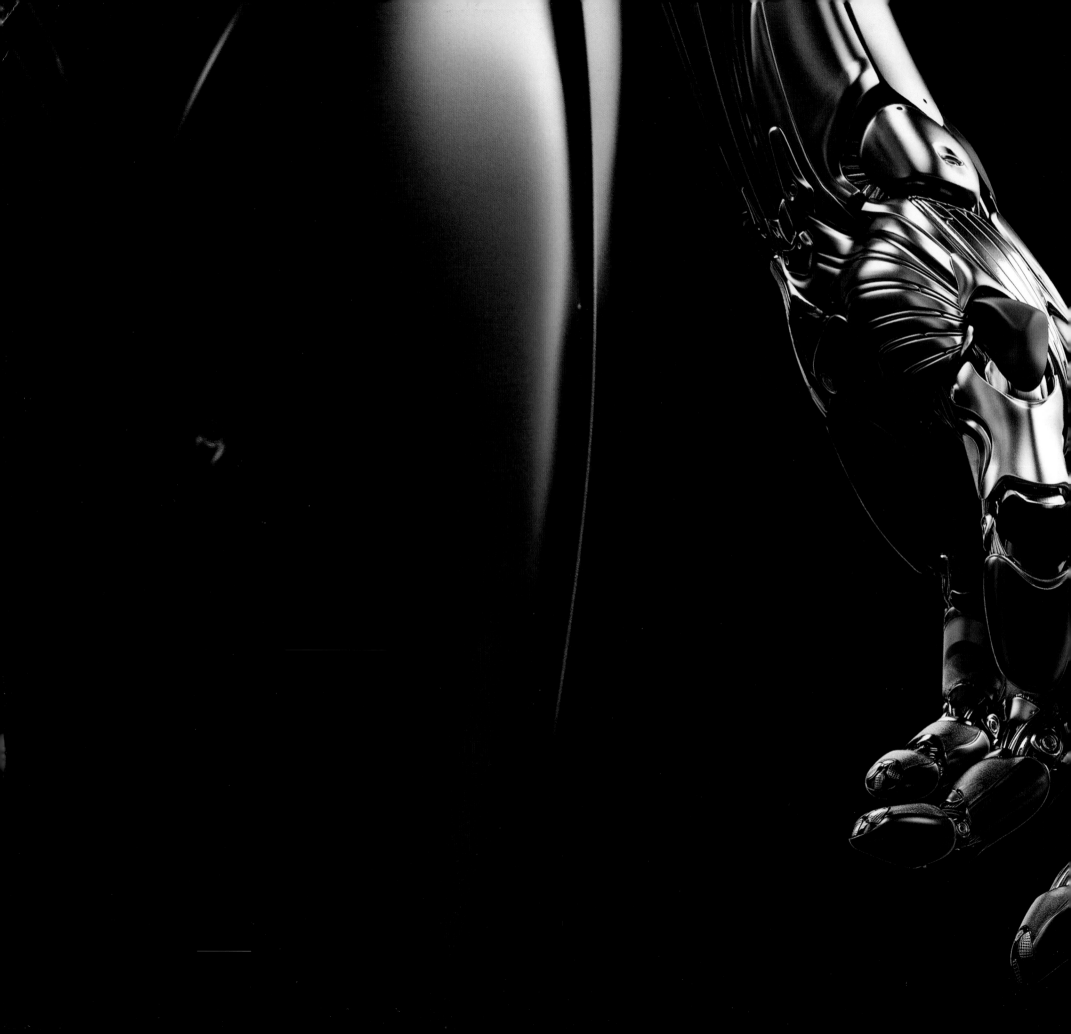

# CONTENTS

# FOREWORD

I began my career as an illustrator, and as a filmmaker I've enjoyed bringing graphic novels to cinematic life. What *Alita* had was the added bonus of being a highly anticipated James Cameron project a decade earlier – one that he had spent a lot of time writing, visualizing, and working out for himself to originally direct. So, getting to work with him to realize the dream of bringing this project to fruition was beyond anything I could have imagined.

To say that working with Jim is like taking years of master classes would be an understatement. He is simply at the top of his craft, and is extremely generous with his time and attention. A fact I found staggering when considering all that he was taking on at the time in launching his *Avatar* films. I loved his eye-opening take on the material, which was to craft a story with the spectacle and high emotional stakes we expect in his films.

*Alita* is the story of discovering your true inner power. It shows how, even if we feel we are not as important as someone else, we can find and tap into an inner strength and purpose and be heroic. Alita wakes up in a world she doesn't know, in a body that isn't hers, and feels out of place and feels insignificant. As she grows to discover love, family, and friendship, those who consider her a threat make her realize her true importance and her true identity and it turns her new world upside down.

It would take an army of technicians and artists to build this world from the ground up. We all had to tap into our own inner power to deliver the level of quality that a Jim Cameron film demands, and yet at the same time give the story it's very own heartbeat.

—Robert Rodriguez, *Director*

**THIS SPREAD:** Concept art of Hugo with Alita in her doll body.

# THE GENESIS OF
# ALITA: BATTLE ANGEL

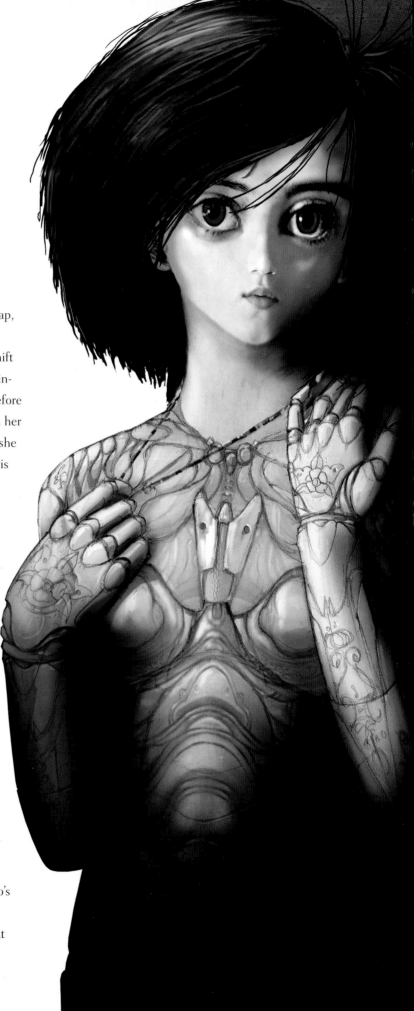

Robert Rodriguez believes that *Alita: Battle Angel* exists as a feature film because he turned around in a parking lot. In early 2015, Rodriguez was in the process of wrapping up what became a four-hour lunch with his friend James Cameron. Cameron, who was working on his four *Avatar* sequels, had shown Rodriguez artwork for the epic projects at Lightstorm's Manhattan Beach, California facility.

"Jim told me that was all he was going to make for the rest of his career, any story he wanted to tell, he would just do through the *Avatar* world," Rodriguez recalls. "So, I was already headed to my car, and I remember saying, 'I have a last question: If you're only going to do *Avatar*, what happens to the other projects you have, like *Alita: Battle Angel*?' And Jim said, 'You got fifteen minutes?'"

Based on the long-running manga by Yukito Kishiro, *Alita: Battle Angel* is set 600 years in the future. The world has been devastated by an interplanetary war that took place three centuries earlier. At its end, refugees gathered below the last of the great Sky Cities, Zalem, and built Iron City. In Iron City, you serve Zalem or you don't live very long. For most people, that means you work for the Factory. Zalem runs the Factory and the Factory runs the town. Pretty much everything that is made in Iron City goes up the supply tubes to the sky people so they can live in luxury above the clouds. In return, they dump their garbage onto the city below.

The ground population has varying degrees of recovered technology, one of which is the ability to make cybernetic enhancements to humans. Most often these enhancements are intended to create more efficient workers. For a select group of athletes, the cybernetic enhancements allow them to compete in the sport of Motorball. A sport created by the Factory to relieve violent tension in Iron City.

When cybersurgeon Dr. Dyson Ido finds the discarded cyber core of a young female in a scrap heap, he is shocked to discover that its very human brain shows signs of life. He brings her back to his makeshift operating room and puts her into a beautiful porcelain-like cyborg body that he had lovingly crafted years before for his own now-deceased daughter. Alita awakens in her new body with no memory of who she was or where she came from. As Alita ventures out into the world, she is determined to find out about her mysterious past.

Cameron explains he had been introduced to *Alita* in its anime film form by his friend and fellow filmmaking legend Guillermo del Toro. "I got a lump in my throat at the end of it. My oldest daughter was quite young at the time and I also saw it as this great female empowerment story."

This inspired Cameron to seek out the original manga. He wanted to make a movie inspired by, as he says, "the richness and the detail in the artwork created by Yukito Kishiro."

In 2000, Lightstorm acquired the feature film rights to *Alita*. Cameron wrote a screenplay; Laeta Kalogridis worked on several drafts. *Alita* producer/Lightstorm COO Jon Landau relates, "We felt that *Alita* had everything that Lightstorm embodies. We want to make movies that have themes that are bigger than their genre. This is a young woman's journey of self-discovery, where she comes into the world viewing herself as someone who's insignificant, but who comes to realizes she has the ability to change the world. I think it's a reminder that

**LEFT & ABOVE:** Early (2005) concept art of Alita in her doll body.

within each one of us is that same ability."

At the same time he was developing the script for *Alita*, technology had advanced to a point where it was conceivable that Lightstorm might finally be able to produce a script Cameron had written years before, *Avatar*. "We knew that we wanted to use performance capture to bring the characters of both *Avatar* and *Alita* to life," says Landau.

"We got to the point where it was literally a coin toss between *Battle Angel* and *Avatar*," Cameron notes. "We thought, 'Let's develop one system of performance capture to create these CG characters. We'll amortize our development costs for the system across two projects, ultimately maybe even two franchises.'"

As Cameron's team built out a system on which to test just how far the boundaries of the then-fledgling performance capture technologies could be pushed, it was decided to actually capture a scene to get a sense of what was possible. Wanting to test the system with a dialogue scene that included two performance-capture characters, Cameron randomly chose to select a scene from *Avatar*. Cameron says, "In the process of bringing the *Avatar* characters to life, we fell in love. So then it wasn't a coin toss anymore, we just never stopped doing *Avatar*. But a couple of days before the test, it could have been either movie on the fast track."

Avatar went into production, and thereafter into box office history, while *Battle Angel* went into limbo

for approximately a decade. Then came Rodriguez's parking-lot query. Cameron showed Rodriguez a video presentation of artwork created in 2005 by an elite group of artists that Cameron had hired. The presentation showcased the art with accompanying voiceover narration, telling the story of what was, at that point, Cameron and Kalogridis' 190-page screenplay. Rodriguez remembers his reaction. "Seeing the artwork, one compelling image after another, and how [Cameron] was going to bring it to life, I decided it looked like the coolest thing ever."

Rodriguez volunteered to see if he could edit the script down by approximately a third. He still recalls Cameron's response: "'If you can crack it, you can direct it.'"

"It's almost like subconsciously I had already decided to hand it off to another filmmaker," Cameron acknowledges, "but only the right filmmaker. It happened in a split second. I thought, 'I would let go of it for Robert.' Because he's got the energy, the creativity, and also a mature talent. He's done CGI-heavy movies, he can handle the action, and I knew he could [create] that almost outrageous sensibility that *Battle Angel* occasionally needs."

"I love reading a script by a director who's also a writer," Rodriguez says. "[Cameron's] is so detailed and so puts you in the movie that you feel like you watched it. He can do all of that design and technical achievement, but he wraps it around a story that everybody loves."

Additionally, "[Cameron] gave me 600 pages of notes. Jim's an engineer. So [his] 600 pages of notes are broken up into categories – [locations, characters], Alita's cyborg tech, what it means to be a cyborg, all the way down the line. That's what really helped me crack the script. He's got such an incredible organizational skill that you have a road map to figure out what he was trying to do."

Rodriguez pared the draft down to 126 pages and then wrote to Cameron. "'There's a plot strand about the Hunter-Warriors, who collect heads. How many heads do I have to collect to work on this great a project?'" Rodriguez laughs. "And Jim wrote back, 'You've collected enough heads.'"

The project also got the blessing of manga author Kishiro, Landau reveals. "I went to Japan and I shared [the screenplay] with Kishiro-san. He was thrilled with what he read, with the art reel, and we even had him come down and visit our set in Austin."

An enormous amount of new concept art was commissioned. *Battle Angel* has unique challenges, specifically making the entirely CGI Alita look photo-realistic next to live actors while preserving her original larger-than-life eyes and proportionately small nose and mouth. Longtime Lightstorm digital effects partner and performance capture expert Weta Digital was chosen for the task. Cameron enthuses, "Weta does the best facial animation, CG animation, the most human, the most alive, the most emotional and the most real of anybody out there."

Although she is CGI, Alita is played by actress Rosa Salazar. Landau feels the term "motion capture" isn't appropriate for the process. "We call it performance capture. I tell people that 'motion capture' is missing one letter in front of it – 'e' for 'emotion.'"

Principal photography was done in late 2016 and early 2017 at Rodriguez's Troublemaker Studios in Austin, Texas. Landau explains, "As Robert will say, 'If you hire a great chef, don't take him out of his kitchen to cook.' We look at Robert as a great chef, and Austin is his kitchen."

**LEFT:** Final still of Alita in her doll body.
**OPPOSITE:** Early (2005) concept art of Alita in her doll body, showing possible costumes.

Rodriguez explains, "I do several kinds of movies. I do *Spy Kids*-type family films. Then I do the other extreme, [violent and sexual] *Machete, Dusk Till Dawn*-type stuff."

With *Sin City* and *From Dusk Till Dawn*, Rodriguez worked in the style of other artists. "*Dusk Till Dawn* was Quentin [Tarantino]'s script, so I was shooting that in a Quentin style. It was almost a way for me to take a vacation from myself, to go do a *Sin City* that was completely Frank Miller's world come to life. You are there more as a facilitator, rather than, 'I'm going to make my vision.'

"For [*Battle Angel*], I wanted to do this more in the style of a Jim Cameron film. Even though he didn't draw every frame, it was as clearly mapped out as *Sin City* was for me, where I could literally just go shoot the book. I wanted *Alita* to feel like it was totally in his world."

Asked to define a quintessential Cameron shot, Rodriguez replies, "There was a shot in *The Terminator* when [the Terminator] is going through the police station, you're looking up, the camera is scraping the ground, and he's walking through the fiery hallway with the two guns in his hands, and it's dark under the boot as he steps over

a body, and then it tilts up, and he's just towering, and you just know that no one's getting out of there alive, that he's unstoppable."

*Battle Angel* uses this style when the villainous Zapan is pursuing Alita's love Hugo. "It's a low angle. You have to time it right so the actor doesn't bump into the camera and move it at a certain speed. You drop that camera low, the audience is just at the mercy of looking up at this guy towering over them, charging, relentless. It looks like its own thing, as he's weaving through people. So it's got a little bit of difference to it, but it's so powerful that it works. There are probably a whole bunch of other types of Jim Cameron shots [in the film]. Where I would tend to do a camera a certain way, his can be very visceral, but then get very elegant, very epic and very slow moves that take in an environment."

Because Rodriguez's previous films have not had *Battle Angel*'s budget, "I would always have to hide [the environment], because I didn't have the production value. I had to always use cuts and long lenses to hide the fact that we didn't have sets. So shooting it like Jim meant I could say, 'Let's really show the scope.' Every shot that

comes in from Weta is like, 'Wow, let's throw a little more light on that. That holds up to any scrutiny."

Cameron says of Rodriguez, "He was always very respectful of what I had written and of the world that Kishiro had created, but he's also not afraid to make it his own, and I wanted to give him as much space as he needed creatively. We fell into this really good working relationship. It turns out that he's insanely collaborative, he really likes the camaraderie of working with other creative people."

The themes of *Alita: Battle Angel* speak to its makers. Like Cameron, Rodriguez was also moved by the father/daughter relationship between Ido and Alita. "My daughter's almost Alita's age. I totally identified with [Ido]. The coolest thing about being a parent is the point where your child can see you in a different way, because your paths are similar enough that they look at you as a mentor now, and as someone who can guide them through life in a direction that they want to go. That's what happens with Ido. When Alita finds out that he's actually a Hunter-Warrior and a badass, she wants to learn from him."

And Rodriguez loves his own learning curve on *Battle Angel*. "I say, 'Always be a student in life and in your work. If you always think like a student, you're free to take chances like a student. Surround yourself by masters in every department and learn from the best.' That's what this experience was for me. I'm really coming in here to learn a great deal from all of these collaborators, from [director of photography] Bill Pope, from [film editor] Steve Rivkin, from all the Weta artists, all the *Avatar* artists, from Jon Landau, who has worked so much and knows how to be a leader and a producer. I'm going in there wide-eyed, like Alita herself, just soaking up this whole world.

"I've worked with my crew for a long time," Rodriguez explains. "Steve Joyner the production designer, Brian Bettwy my first AD [assistant director], these are people that were on the set of *Dusk Till Dawn* back in '95. Jim said to us all, 'You go make this movie,' and we graduated to another level. It put a spring in everyone's step and upped everyone's game.

"It was freaking incredible to see all that we had worked for over the years – our scrappy version of 3D before anybody was doing it, with greenscreen, digital photography, all the stuff that we were pioneering in our own way down in Austin – coming to fruition. By being outside of Hollywood, we could think differently with it. That mindset is what gave Jim the trust to let us go ahead and make this movie," Rodriguez concludes. "To work with somebody who was such a friend over twenty-two years, and a mentor, somebody that I am a huge fan of, and to go make a Jim-style movie with his army of artists, and then for Jim to turn around and say that he loves the movie, that's the best feeling."

**RIGHT:** Concept art of Alita in her Berserker body.
**FAR RIGHT:** Alita finds the Berserker body inside the crashed URM warship.

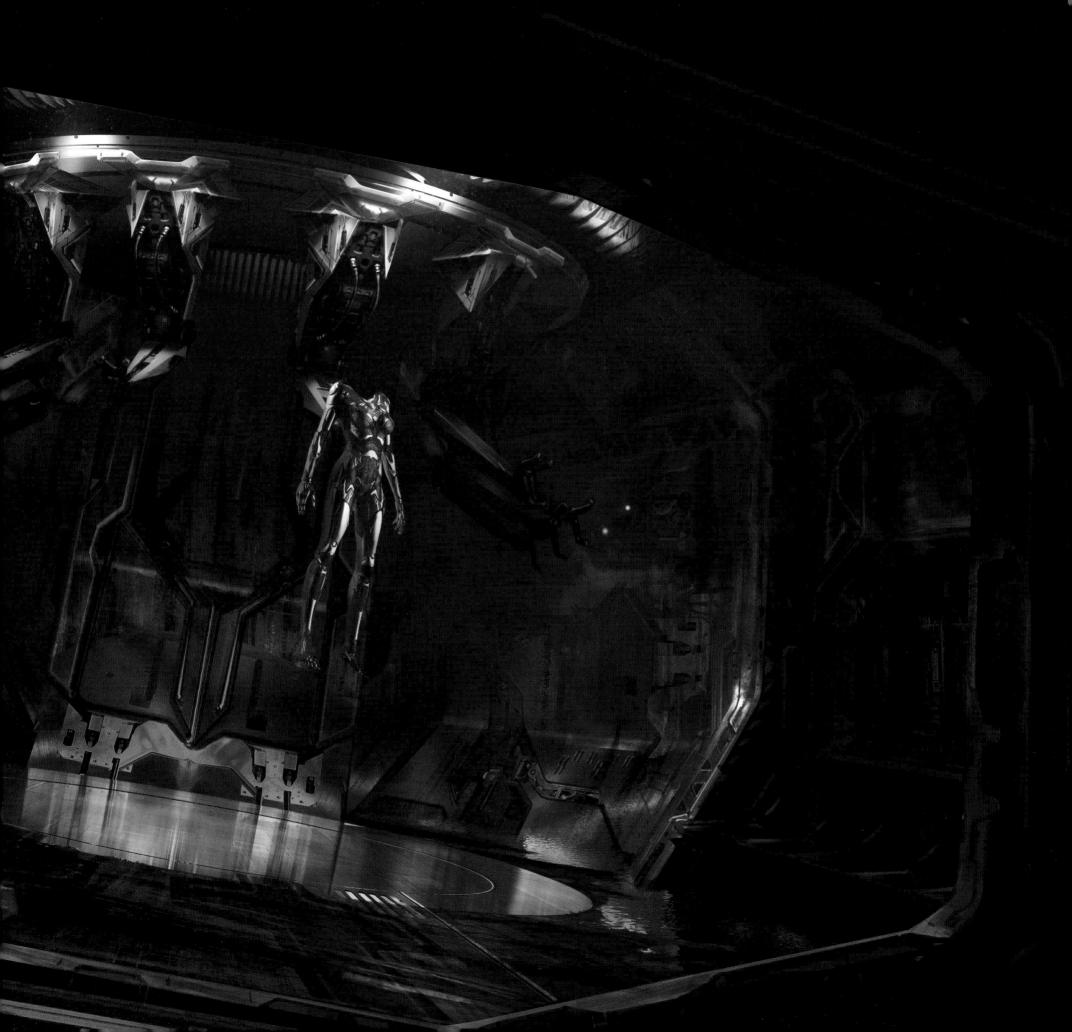

**THIS SPREAD:** Concept art of Alita gearing up in the locker room for her Motorball tryout as Ido watches anxiously.

# ALITA

"This movie is the story of Alita's journey toward a better understanding of her own identity," James Cameron says. "I like Alita because she's absolutely fearless. When she's confronted with an injustice, she will do something. Her vulnerability is about the people she loves – she will never fear for herself, [only] for them."

"We see the world through Alita's eyes," producer Jon Landau explains. "She comes into it not expecting anything. She's just taking everything in. That's what we want the audience to do."

Alita goes through several transitions, both psychological and physical. Her cyber core is found in the Iron City Scrapyard by Dr. Dyson Ido, who puts it into the beautifully hand-crafted cyborg body he had previously built for his now-deceased daughter. After Alita's Cybergirl form, or "doll body," is devastated in a fight, Ido transfers her core into an URM (United Republic of Mars) Berserker body, the most advanced cyborg weapon ever created, which adapts its form to her.

While all versions of Alita were portrayed in performance capture by Rosa Salazar, onscreen, Alita is completely CGI, though she looks photo-realistic and interacts with live actors around her. So *Battle Angel* required extremely close collaboration between the visual effects designers at Lightstorm in Southern California and 3D animators at Weta Digital in New Zealand. "It's all about if you can make the audience

**THIS PAGE:** Concept art of Alita's cyber core, as Ido finds it in the Scrapyard.

**ABOVE:** Early (2005) concept art of Alita's cyber core, as Ido finds it in the Scrapyard.    **ABOVE RIGHT:** Weta Digital model of Alita's cyber core, as Ido finds it in the Scrapyard.

believe that character's real in a tight close-up," observes Cameron. "Rosa Salazar is our greatest asset on this movie. It's hard to quantify how big the reaction was [during the audition] that Robert [Rodriguez] and I both had to Rosa's performance."

*Alita*'s Weta senior visual effects supervisor Joe Letteri explains that his team is combining imagery inspired by the original manga, artwork developed from 2005 on for the project, and Salazar's performance, which "is what we ground the character in. Alita has a heart-shaped face with a small mouth and very large eyes. So we started working out animation studies with Rosa's features and put them into those shapes. [Alita's] mouth still resembles Rosa's, her eyes still resemble Rosa's, but we had to make a lot of changes to accommodate the fact that, for example, Alita's mouth is

so small. It means her jaw is a little bit smaller. Similarly, the big eyes have to fit into enlarged sockets. But if you build the underlying eye sockets and everything that supports the eye, and get all the detail right, then your mind will take it in believably."

Letteri continues, "We have to build Alita's three-dimensional model in the computer. It's like a moving sculpture. We have a skull inside of this model for the

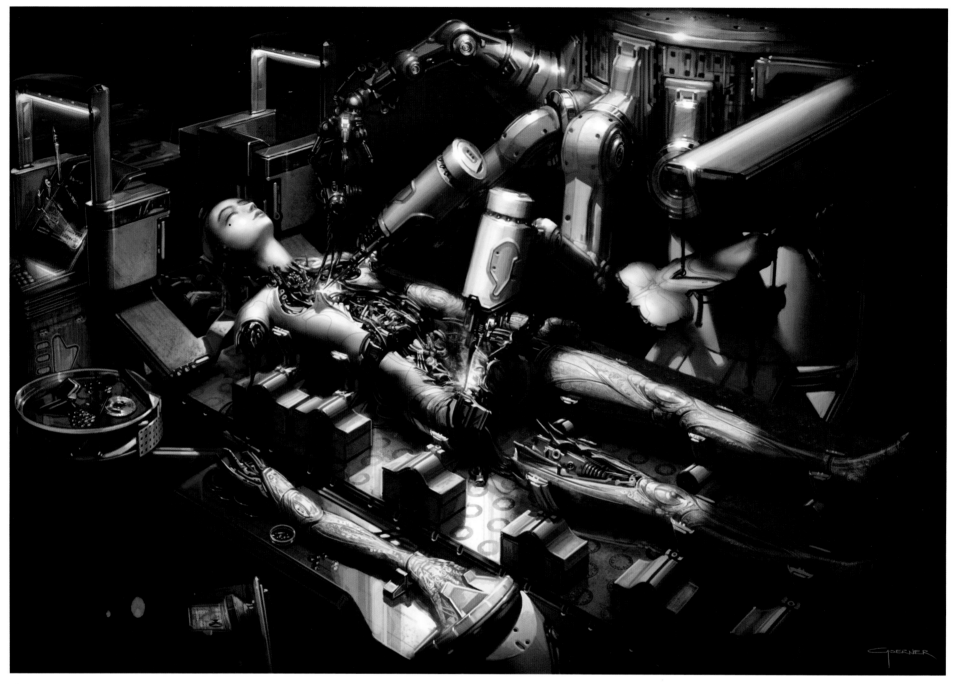

**ABOVE:** Early (2005) concept art of Alita's cyber core being placed into her doll body.    **RIGHT:** Concept art of Alita in her doll body.

articulation." When Alita changes bodies, "We have to change the shape of the skull slightly. Her face changes to reflect the older character that she becomes: the shape is a little more oval, the nose gets a little stronger, the cheekbones become a little more pronounced. The skull changes to reflect what you're seeing on the face outside."

Character designer Joe Pepe says his initial job on *Battle Angel* was to help generate different variants of Alita's eye, mouth and nose sizes. Though he can't confirm exactly how much larger Alita's eyes are compared to normal human eyes at the time of writing, experiments went from twelve to forty-five percent

larger, with her nose and mouth reduced by as much as twelve-and-a-half percent smaller than human, "just to see if it worked or not. Jim always says, 'Take it to the point of breaking it.'

"On the first image," Pepe continues, "everybody had their ideal version of what they wanted." This started with input from director Rodriguez, then went to Cameron. "I did versions based on the two of them speaking to one another." Pepe then gathered input from visual consultants Ben Procter and Dylan Cole, and had his own ideas as well. Rodriguez also sent some of his favorite images from the manga. "Robert was doing a little Photoshop," Pepe recalls. "He would take my artwork and liquefy and draw on it, and send it back. Even if I had followed the initial notes, sometimes it looks a little different than you had expected, so he got hands-on with that."

Visual effects supervisor Richard E. Hollander

was tasked with making sure that the agreed-upon art concepts look three-dimensional and move accordingly. "I would say the mouth is the hardest thing to do, followed by the eyes. The proportions of Alita's head are slightly altered. Getting that sculpturally to look good involved quite a bit of trial and error. Even after you build these characters, you have to keep adjusting them."

Weta visual effects supervisor Eric Saindon reveals that the initial artwork of Alita's cyber core was done by Procter. "We built our model based on that, and then we added roughening and patina to make her feel like she fit into the Scrapyard where Ido finds her body, [where] all

the metal is similarly distressed. We've given her the same effect. Her core was scuffed and worn down, so that it looks like she could have been there for a long time."

Procter in turn credits "genius 3D designer Vitaly Bulgarov" with doing a lot of concept art on Alita's original form, which was "heavily influenced by the original manga. There were one or two images in particular that really guided it. In 2005, [concept artist] James Clyne did a black and white illustration of Alita in a casual ball position. We owe a debt to a lot of work those [original concept artists] did."

For the texture of Alita's doll body, Procter says that

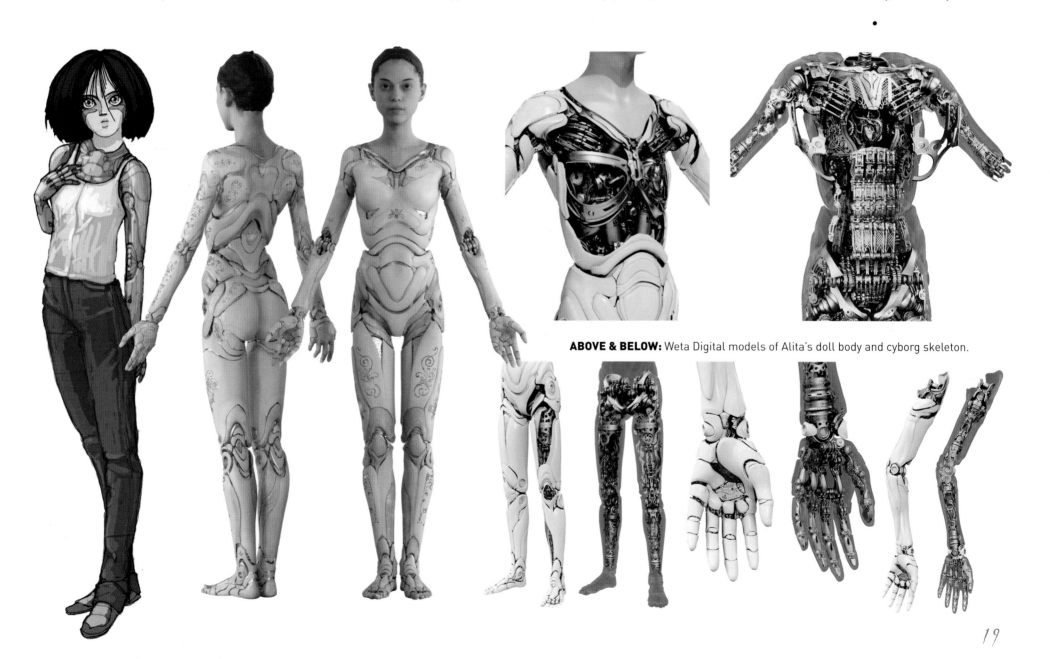

**ABOVE & BELOW:** Weta Digital models of Alita's doll body and cyborg skeleton.

19

Rodriguez provided a screengrab of an alabaster vase from the 1987 movie *Angel Heart*. "We were looking at that, combined with this decorative etching [on the body], combined with slightly steampunky brass details for how the joints worked." The computer combined precise percentages of photo-reference material to achieve the final texture, but Procter cautions, "I don't want to give too much credit to the computer, because it's people hand-making texture maps, and choosing what photographic sources to use. What we went for material-wise is something that's probably a resin, a plastic, but it reads both as slightly porcelain and slightly alabaster. So it's got more specular breakup, which is the way that highlights look on something, little pings of light."

In contrast, the Berserker body costume is dark, but "It's very reflective," Saindon notes. "There are parts of it that are metal, and other parts that are almost translucent silicone, which gives her a whole other level

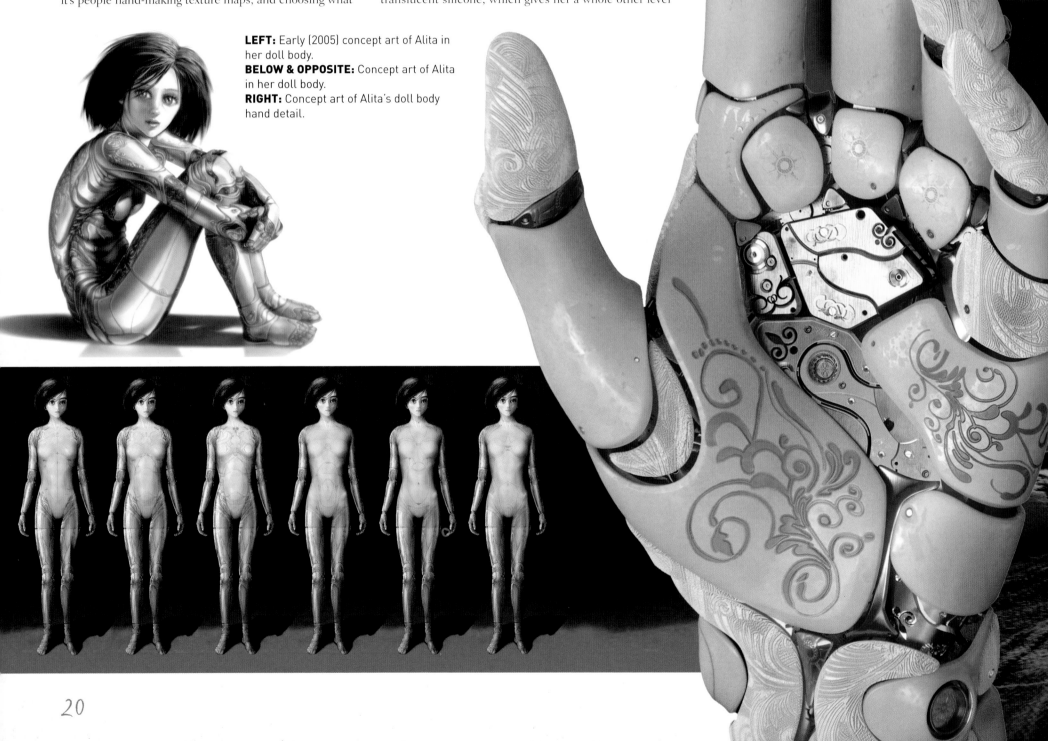

**LEFT:** Early (2005) concept art of Alita in her doll body.
**BELOW & OPPOSITE:** Concept art of Alita in her doll body.
**RIGHT:** Concept art of Alita's doll body hand detail.

of depth. You see into her muscles a little, you get different levels of skin, because as you see into her muscle, you also see the bones within her muscle."

For Alita's height, Saindon explains, "Cybergirl is around five-foot-one, Rosa is closer to five-foot-two, and Berserker is almost five-foot-four. So, because Rosa fits right in between, we can take her motion and get the motion for both Alitas. When Rosa was Cybergirl, her movements were a little bit more innocent. When she was Berserker, she became much more confident and strong. We don't have to do a lot to those performances. We create [each form in the computer] and then we put a skeleton in it, and that skeleton is driven by Rosa's performance, so that as Rosa moves our 3D geometry moves around with it."

Longtime Rodriguez costume designer Nina Proctor was in charge of the physical, practical costumes created at Troublemaker Studios. She describes Alita's Cybergirl wardrobe as that of "a soft, cool fourteen-year-old. She's wearing pants and T-shirts. [Salazar's] photo double was dressed in her clothes, and she would do a little bit of the action, so we could see how the clothes moved. Then Weta Digital photographed everything – front, back, sides. Anything that we custom-built, we made them sets of patterns, so when they're painting it in, they're able to follow our patterns."

**BELOW & RIGHT:** Concept art of Alita in her doll body.

"I went with softer colors, thin jackets – we're at the equator, so it can't be anything real heavy. As Alita progresses, we get her into boots rather than high-top tennis shoes and as she gets to know this group of kids, we make her a little bit more stylish; fitted cargo pants, shorter T-shirts. We were careful about her necklines – some of those choices were to help with the CGI process, because the costume was so close to the face." Any material with a softer, less defined edge would make the CGI process more complicated.

When Alita enters the rough Kansas Bar, Proctor says, "We make her look tougher there through the kind of boot that she has on. They are a little bit taller than ankle boots, lace-ups, but then they have several straps of leather that wrap around the boot."

For Alita's Berserker body, Proctor says, "I custom made a black leather bodysuit that was really fitted, and then all of these pieces for her arms will be painted in over that."

The scene where Alita literally offers Hugo her heart, removing the organ from her chest, called for special planning, Proctor recalls. "I wanted to emphasize that our young Alita [is] now an eighteen-year-old, with a cute top that is a little bit fitted and cap sleeves that really show off her new arms. And with a zipper front, so that when we get to the part where she tells Hugo, 'Here, you can have my heart,' she simply has to unzip a little bit, and she can pull her heart out. She's not trying to pull a T-shirt over

**BELOW:** Alita's doll body destroyed.
**RIGHT:** Concept art of Alita in her doll body.

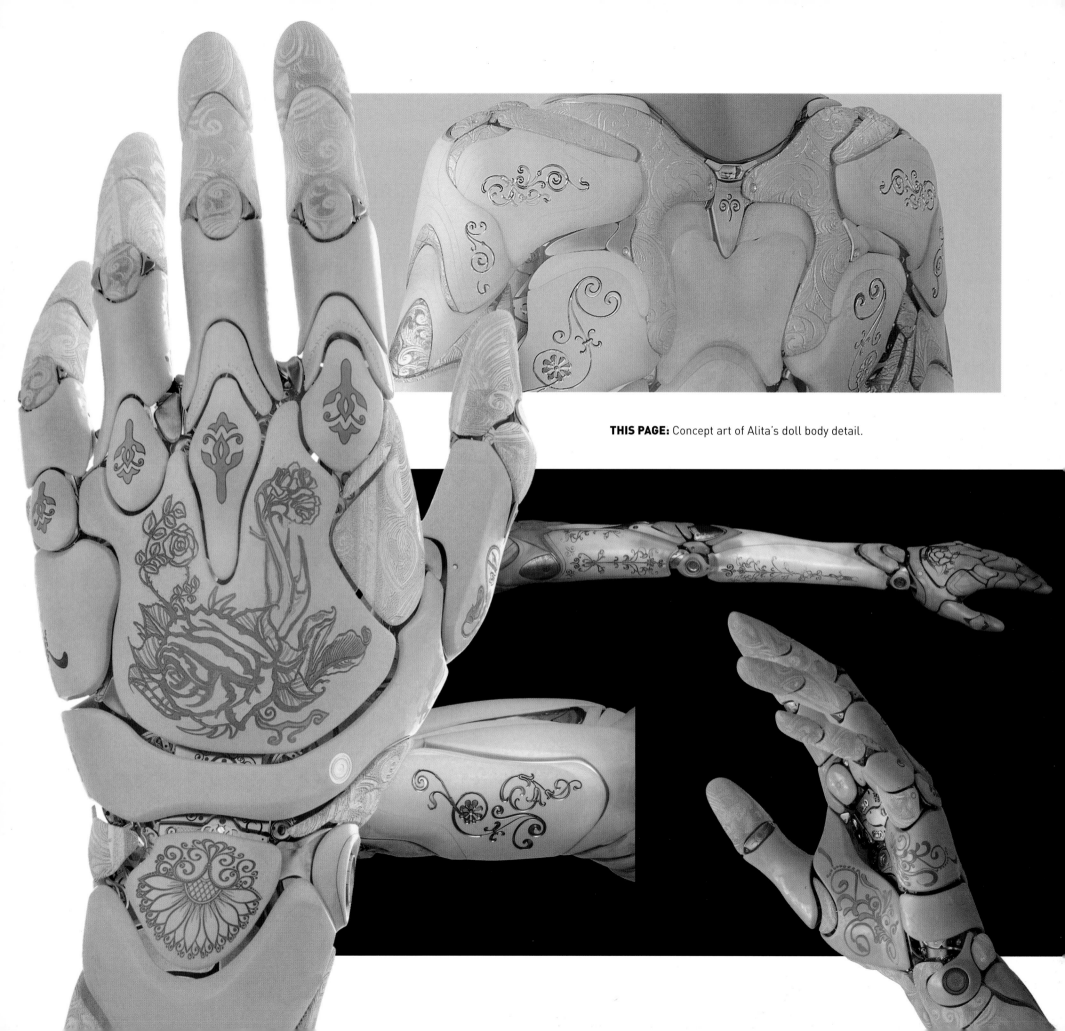

**THIS PAGE:** Concept art of Alita's doll body detail.

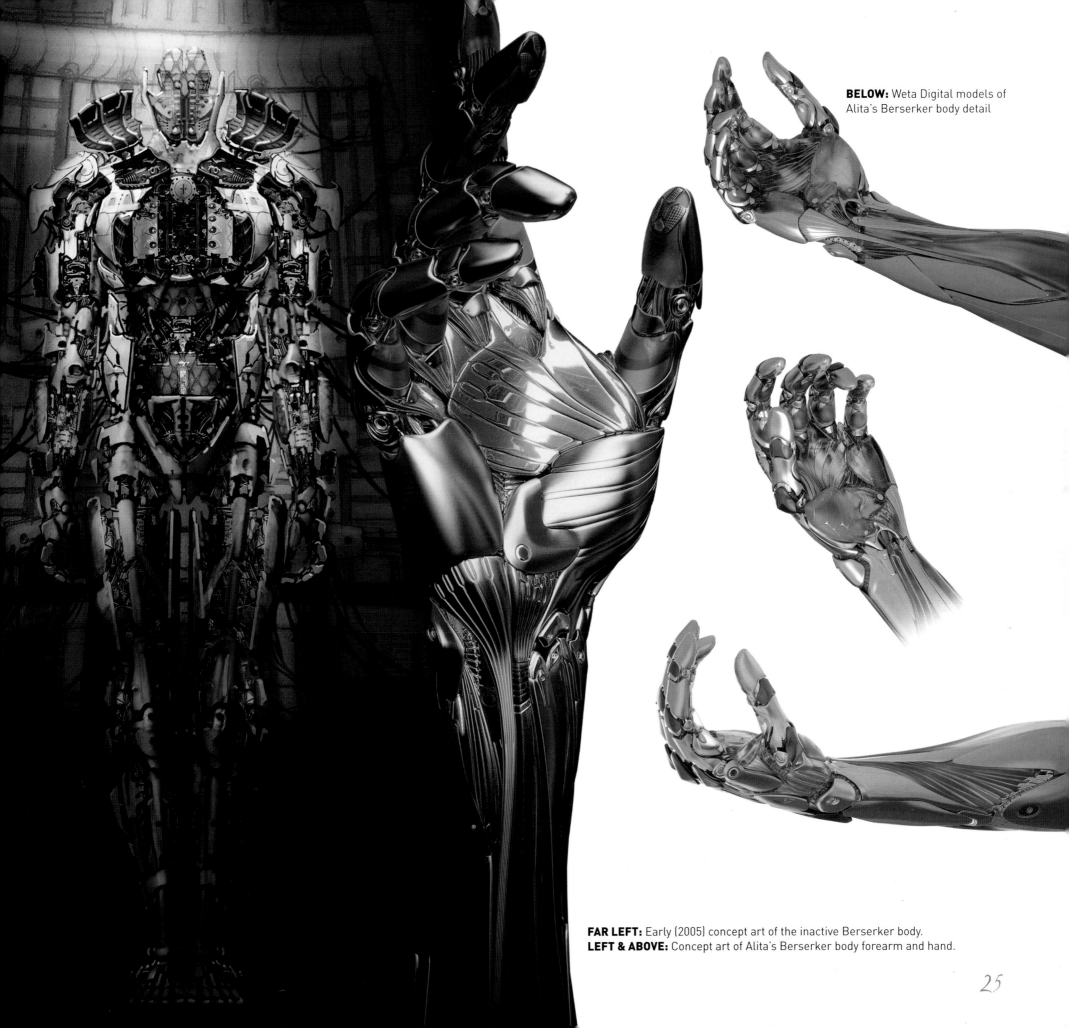

**BELOW:** Weta Digital models of Alita's Berserker body detail

**FAR LEFT:** Early (2005) concept art of the inactive Berserker body.
**LEFT & ABOVE:** Concept art of Alita's Berserker body forearm and hand.

**LEFT:** Concept art of Alita in her Berserker body.
**ABOVE:** Concept art of Alita's cyber core being placed into her Berserker body.

her head, or messing with buttons."

"Weta did a full-scale 3D printout of Alita," Saindon recalls, "and we gave that to [digital costume consultant] Deborah Scott. Deb did her actual costumes on that printout. She built them to the scale she wanted out of the material she wanted, and then we found a thirteen-year-old girl with the exact same proportions and the exact same height as the 3D printout. We put those costumes on her, and we were able to walk her around and film her, so that we could see the movement of the cloth, how it draped, the way it moved when she did different motions. Then we took Deb's sewing patterns and built those same patterns in 3D space, [using] a

technology called Marvelous Designer."

Scott worked on Alita's wardrobe at Lightstorm and describes her work on *Battle Angel* as "Refining things, so that the digital world could in some ways enhance the costumes that were laid out for Alita, because while they're shooting, Salazar's almost always wearing a performance-capture suit, so you never really get to see her in her wardrobe. Our approach enabled us to solve a lot of technical problems, as well as make either color changes or variations on the original costume.

"For instance," Scott elaborates, "as they start developing the body design digitally, they may consequently want to go back and redesign some of

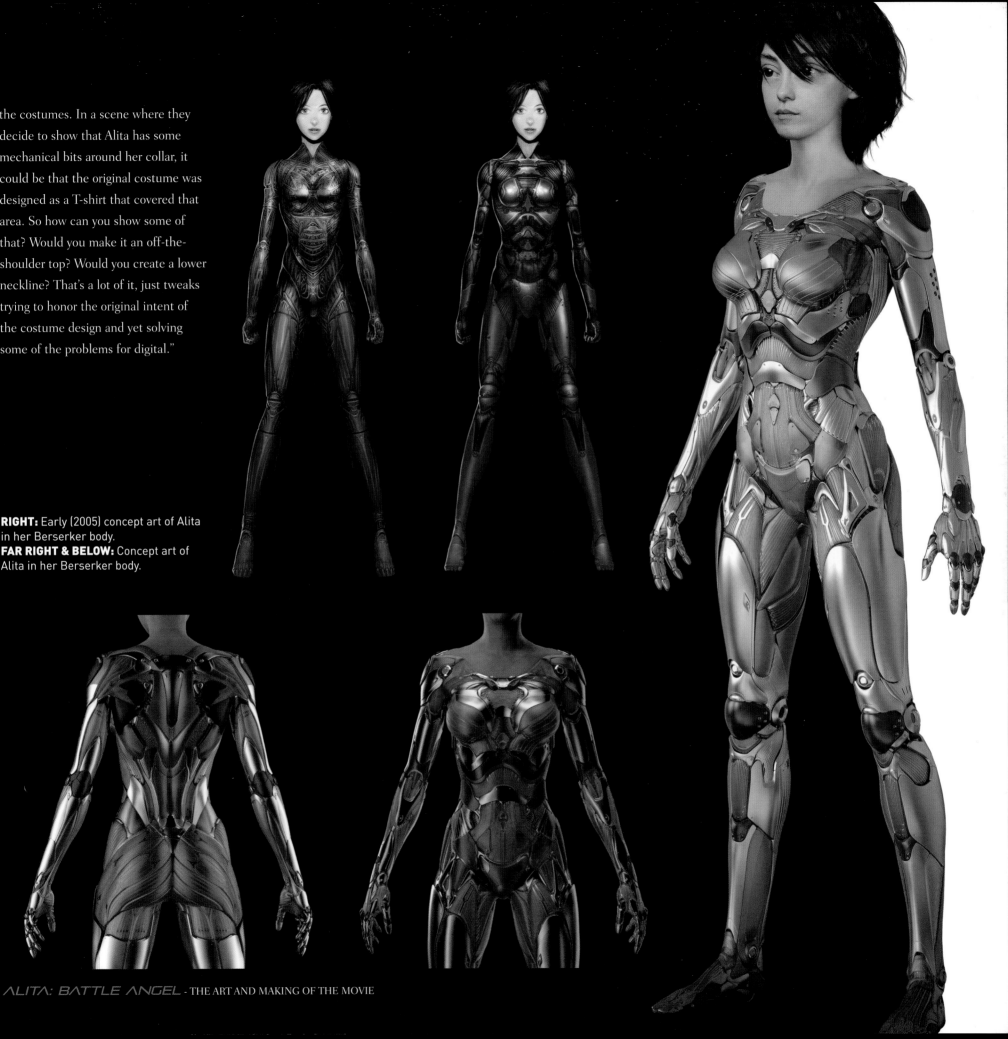

the costumes. In a scene where they decide to show that Alita has some mechanical bits around her collar, it could be that the original costume was designed as a T-shirt that covered that area. So how can you show some of that? Would you make it an off-the-shoulder top? Would you create a lower neckline? That's a lot of it, just tweaks trying to honor the original intent of the costume design and yet solving some of the problems for digital."

**RIGHT:** Early (2005) concept art of Alita in her Berserker body.
**FAR RIGHT & BELOW:** Concept art of Alita in her Berserker body.

**LEFT:** Early (2005) concept art of Alita in her Berserker body.
**ABOVE:** Concept art of Alita in her Berserker body.
**BELOW:** Concept art of Alita in her Berserker body and with the Damascus Blade.

**ABOVE & RIGHT:** Early (2005) concept art of Alita in her professional Motorball body with the Damascus Blade.
**BELOW:** Concept art of Alita at her Motorball tryout.

Those digital challenges, director Robert Rodriguez enthuses, are a big part of why he wanted to bring the Alita character to life. When he viewed Cameron's 2005 *Battle Angel* artwork of Alita, Rodriguez says, "I saw that he was going for a true anime character that we've never seen live-action photo-real. That was really what inspired me to take it on, because I thought, 'Wow, that's something that I hadn't seen, and we could write the book on what that looks like.' Rosa was so expressive, you were picturing how amazing the animated version would look of what she was doing."

**ABOVE & OPPOSITE TOP:** Concept art of Alita's various wheel feet for street, tryout and professional Motorball.
**BELOW:** Concept art of Alita's Motorball tryout.

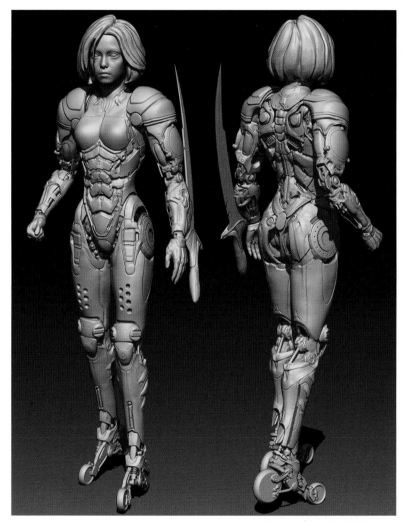

**ABOVE:** Concept art of Alita in her professional Motorball body.
**FAR LEFT:** Photo of practical wheel feet prop.
**LEFT:** Concept art of Alita in her Motorball tryout helmet.

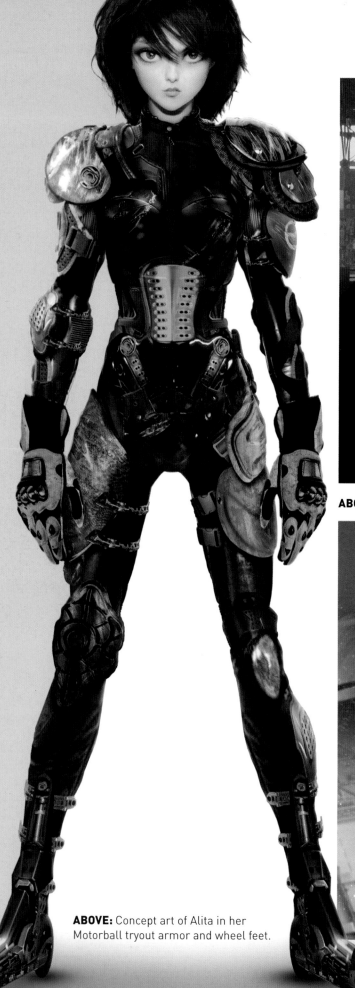

**ABOVE & BELOW:** Concept art of Alita in her professional Motorball body, wielding the Damascus Blade.

**ABOVE:** Concept art of Alita in her Motorball tryout armor and wheel feet.

# ALITA'S HEART

"Our cyborgs fit into two clean categories: TRs – Total Replacements – and partial replacements," visual consultant Ben Procter points out. Alita is a TR, meaning she has an entirely machine body and one irreplaceable element, "The cyber core, which consists of a human brain, some representation of a skull to protect the brain, all the plumbing of life support, and connected to that, a thoracic cavity containing artificial organs that perform the functions of the lungs and heart, and pump both cyber blood and human blood. The brain is the only thing that requires human blood, which is red. Everything else is blue cyber blood.

"One element of Alita's heart is some sort of matter/antimatter power reactor," Procter continues. "That is part of the Berserker power. She can move her body using actuators or the muscles with such force that it doesn't matter that she doesn't weigh that much. In fact, a significant proportion of her body weight overall is the heart. Jim [Cameron] wrote notes about it – it's some sort of mono-molecular housing that weighs about three hundred pounds, even though it's relatively small."

Production designer Steve Joyner has a physical version of Alita's heart sitting on his office shelf. "That was designed by Vitaly Bulgarov, the wonderful 3D designer," he says, "and it will be realized in CG by Weta. Rosa performed on set with a grey 3D printed version from Vitaly's artwork that I now have. It's going to look great in the movie when Weta's done with it."

**TOP RIGHT:** Concept art of Alita offering Hugo her heart.
**BELOW & RIGHT:** 3D concept design of Alita's heart.

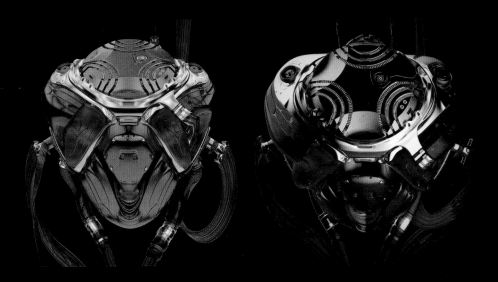

# DAMASCUS BLADE

The most powerful weapon in *Alita: Battle Angel* is Alita herself. She has memories of the Panzer Kunst fighting style, which Robert Rodriguez describes as what "the elite force of [cyborg] Berserkers were trained in. She can go into this mode where she's using what has been a lost fighting art for 300 years. To create Panzer Kunst, I got to work with stunt coordinator Garrett Warren. He's fantastic at coming up with what these moves would be and designing a mix of different martial arts styles to pull that off. I worked with him briefly on *Sin City*. I've known him over the years – great energy, always inventive, great team. I'm an action guy, so getting to work with guys like Garrett is always fun."

The cyborg Berserker body has some unique powers of its own. "The signature folds that [the body] has on the inside of the biceps emit a plasma corona that wraps around Alita's arm and snakes down onto the Damascus Blade," visual consultant Ben Procter explains, "which is powered or superheated by plasma that the Berserker body itself emits."

The Damascus Blade is a Berserker sword that has found its way into Hunter-Warrior Zapan's possession. "The sword is of URM manufacture," confirms production designer Steve Joyner. "Zapan doesn't necessarily know this. Alita realizes that she has some sort of connection with that sword, defeats Zapan and takes the sword."

There were a number of different production versions of the sword. "Rosa Salazar as Alita and Ed Skrein as Zapan use the same weight sword, but often, depending on what they were doing, they would use just the hilt," Joyner says. "We had several aluminum swords, wooden ones, rubber ones, and hilt-only swords." The hilt is also of URM origin. "We built ours out of aluminum and gave it a matte but slightly iridescent paint finish."

**ABOVE:** Concept art of the Damascus Blade.
**RIGHT:** Concept art of Alita in her Berserker body with the Damascus Blade.

"There is a lot of the sword in the original manga," Joyner explains, describing the development process for the Damascus Blade. "So we were looking at a traditional sword, but adding some high-tech elements to it. The shape is unique. It's not a claymore, it's not a katana. It's got elements of everything. Then, in the concept art, one of the artists had done a beautiful circuitry pattern in the hilt, and that's what really made it feel like this plasma weapon that it becomes when Alita wields it. Fabricator Kit Casati developed a process that involved taking the graphic and creating a pattern and then acid-etching, actually engraving the sword with this pattern in an acid bath. The pattern is cut from a vinyl material and applied very carefully by the fabricators, and then they soak the blade in acid overnight, and then Kit pulls it out, cleans it up and polishes it.

"When Jim Cameron picked up the sword, he went into a ten-minute choreography with it," Joyner adds. "He loved it. Kit ended up making five more copies of the sword as wrap presents for the producers and Rosa and Robert."

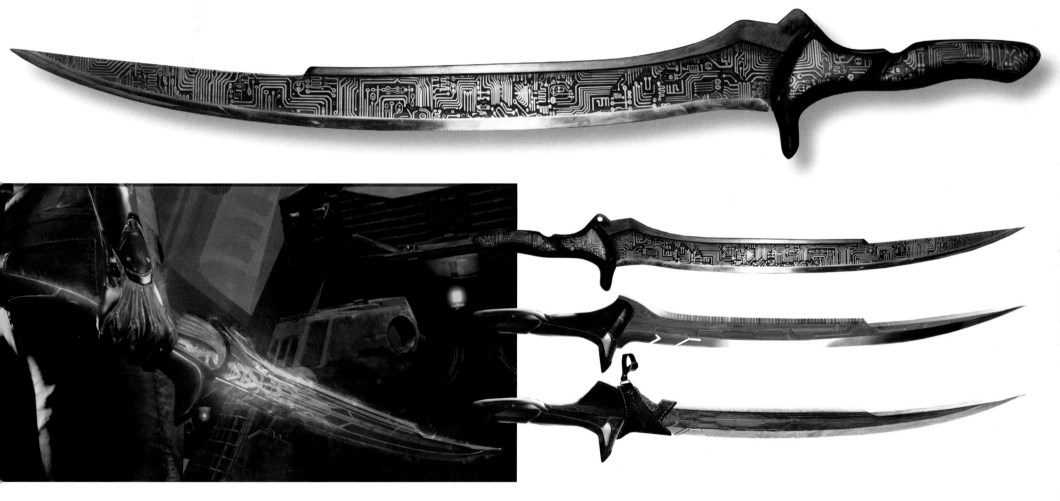

**TOP:** The final concept for the Damascus Blade.
**ABOVE:** Final digital render of the Damascus Blade with plasma corona.

**ABOVE:** Concept art of the Damascus Blade.
**BELOW:** Damascus Blade pattern and photo showing detail of the final sword.

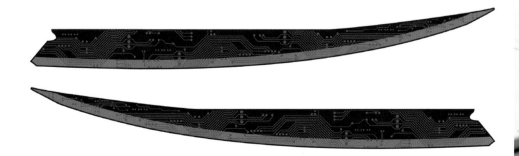

# BRINGING ALITA TO LIFE

Although *Alita: Battle Angel* will be released at the end of 2018 and the first *Avatar* film came out in 2009, Lightstorm Entertainment began early development work on both projects at the same time. Each influenced the other, says producer Jon Landau. "When we first started doing *Avatar*, we knew about *Alita*, and we thought that *Avatar* would really benefit *Alita* in the facial performance capture technologies that we were developing for it. Now, having produced *Alita*, I've learned that the reverse will also happen and the *Avatar* sequels will benefit from new technologies and processes we and Weta developed to bring Alita to life."

Even so, the universes of *Alita* and *Avatar* are very different. As Landau points out, "On *Avatar*, so much of what we create with the performances is in a completely virtual world. That's one set of challenges. A whole different level challenge is bringing performance capture characters to life in a live-action set, having them interact with other actors, with animals, and the world. We have to realize their character with CGI that lives up to the photographic reality of a physical set. That's one of the different challenges on *Alita* that we only had to deal with in small parts on the first *Avatar*. On the *Avatar* sequels, we'll deal with that in a much greater percentage of the film. So, what we learned on *Alita* is going to be a real benefit."

One thing that makes *Alita: Battle Angel* unique is that it is the first film to have a completely humanoid but CGI-realized lead interacting with physical surroundings. Alita, played by Rosa Salazar in performance capture translated into CGI, interacts with live-action humans, sets and props. *Alita* exists in a singular space, Landau explains. "Think of visual effects as a bell curve. On one side of it you have all live-action, then you get to the apex where it's visual effects and live-action combined, and then you come back down to all visual effects. *Alita* is landing on the peak of that bell curve, which is the point of most complexity. We are right at the peak of integrating live-action and CGI. The biggest technical challenge on *Alita* is the facial performances. Movies are made in the close-ups. So, what Weta Digital did is create a CGI 1:1 model of Rosa Salazar, so that we can look [at Salazar's live work] side by side [with the digital version] and make sure that we are getting one hundred percent of her performance in the CGI world. Once we knew we had that, that performance could then be translated onto the character of Alita that facially is different, but we knew we were getting Rosa's performance because we had the 1:1 CGI comparison.

"When we were designing Alita," Landau adds, "we thought we really had an opportunity for the first time ever to bring to life, off the pages of a manga, a character that would hold true visually to the manga style. That's why we chose to go with the larger eyes. That's why we chose to go with the smaller mouth. This was all done through a very deliberate and time-consuming development art project where we looked at bigger eyes, smaller eyes, bigger mouths, smaller mouths, bigger head, different hairstyles, all to determine how we could best bring her to life in an emotive and engaging way and still be true to the manga. That was one of our challenges and one of the things that the team of artists that we were lucky enough to have working with us achieved very successfully."

Weta senior visual effects supervisor Joe Letteri explains, "We preserved Alita's oversized eyes from her manga origins, but without breaking from the realism of the world she is in." As Alita also has a cybernetic body, "This balance of large expressive eyes became a key part of her design that helped her character straddle the line between human and machine."

*Alita*'s protagonist is different – and arguably more challenging – because unlike, say, Caesar in the *Planet of the Apes* films, she looks almost entirely human, and unlike the Na'vi characters in the *Avatar* films, the majority of the time she interacts with a practical rather than CG environment. "*Alita* is pretty distinct in the sense that this is the only film where the lead is completely computer generated throughout the entire film – and not an ape – appearing almost entirely in live-action environments," visual effects supervisor Richard Hollander points out. "I've developed other characters in the past, and in doing so you go through a lot of questions. As a character moves further away from human, the questions and objections diminish; the viewer is more forgiving and it ultimately works. But when you get to something that's anthropomorphically closer to human, it's more difficult [to satisfy human perception of that]. I loved the process, asking those questions: What do we put into Alita? What don't we put into Alita? You have this character and you think you know what she's supposed to do. A pure CG solution gives you a lot of flexibility, but you can't do all of those things and stay true to the character. You have to narrow it down and make decisions about how she's going to act, what things you can do to her, before you take it out of Rosa's performance."

Letteri affirms, "Alita was one of the most ambitious characters that Weta Digital has ever created. In 2018, when AI and technology advancements are all over the news, creating a leading character that is equal parts young woman and machine meant that we had to stay true to her emotions as she comes to terms with who she is and begins to forge her own identity. Alita is a multi-dimensional character who is equally at home in a

**OPPOSITE:** Final still of Alita.
**ABOVE:** Rosa Salazar on set in her all-new performance capture suit.

dystopian action scene as she is in a romantic encounter with a new boyfriend."

Weta Digital visual effects supervisor Eric Saindon agrees. "One of the first and most important things with bringing Alita to life was being able to capture Rosa Salazar's entire performance. Capturing Rosa's basic motion was an easy task and not what we were aiming for with Alita. Our goal for this movie was to gather Rosa's every subtle motion, voluntary or not, to elevate Alita from a CG character to an *actor*."

However, Saindon points out, most actors show up at their call time and simply go through wardrobe and makeup before starting the day's shoot. "Rosa's daily routine required her to be with Weta Digital's performance capture team two hours before filming started every day. For this film, we built an all-new performance capture suit specially designed for Rosa. It had all the wires and white balls, commonly seen on motion capture suits, built into the garment. With this suit we were able to capture all of her movement, even her breathing while she performed.

"Before filming started," Saindon explains, "we performed a 3D facial scan of Rosa and printed a fitted mask to help us with the capture dots we applied to her face. By putting holes in the mask, we were able to place the dots in the same place on Rosa's face every day. Connected to her helmet were two small cameras positioned in front of her face, so we could record the change in the dots and her facial performance for every setup while filming. In post-production we would use this footage to determine the exact muscles that were firing in Rosa's face for each frame of the film."

"Actress Rosa Salazar's rich performance gave us a glimpse into Alita's inner feelings, and capturing the emotions in her face was crucial to making Alita come alive," adds Letteri.

Making Alita come alive required not only the all-encompassing performance capture, Letteri continues, but changing the way the effects team approached some aspects of the digital program. "We introduced a new workflow into our facial system to make sure that all of the details of Rosa's feelings and expressiveness

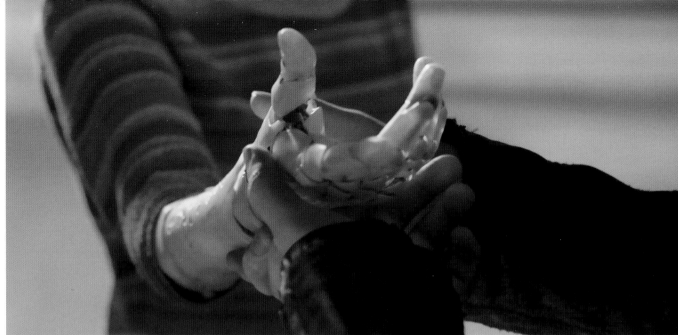

**BELOW & RIGHT:** Filming a scene with Alita and Hugo (Keean Johnson) and a final still from the same scene.

translated to Alita. We built an exact digital replica of Rosa as a validation step between the captured performance and the digital character, so that we could confirm the digital translation of Rosa's facial performance to Alita was exact. This was a level of complexity beyond what we had previously done with Neytiri from *Avatar* or Caesar from *Planet of the Apes*."

As for Lightstorm and Weta joining forces to create Alita, "Who better to pair to make this film, to jump to this level," Hollander says. "Weta and Joe Letteri and the gang already had a lot of experience of what it was like on the *Apes* films. They just kept doing better and better work as time went on. You've got this perfect set-up, and then you have this unique environment. I knew about the technology, but just being around it is different. There's the day-to-day aspect of it, like the facial camera sitting right in front of Rosa." Hollander points out that Salazar quickly adapted to the close proximity of multiple lenses. "We're very interested in shooting with reference cams, pointing five or six cameras at her body and face, that are used as reference for Weta and for the editors."

This, Hollander explains, is to make sure that there is coverage of the performance from all angles, so that the filmmakers can see all possibilities. "The other cameras get that for us. We'd always place one off to the side." Still, *Alita* has been a steep learning curve. "As I proceeded to be involved in this, you

learn what to do, and now I want to make the whole film again," Hollander says. "But that whole process of understanding what you're capturing is incredibly important for doing the edit of the film. You need something there to cut to. This is all practiced behavior in Lightstorm's case. They've been doing this since *Avatar* and are currently producing the next *Avatar*.

"You can't conceptualize your movie unless you have all these parts, including the parts that don't exist [on set] and are going to be CG," Hollander continues. "We used actual elements of Rosa Salazar in her performance capture and that was cut into the film. So we began making the film without our computer-generated Alita. Rosa then begins to get replaced by these different forms. But if you don't have that basis, you can't edit it, and if you don't have some of the reference cameras it makes it really difficult to understand what kind of performance you're going to get. So you do picture-in-picture with her face, to understand how to creatively put together your film. These are really impressive practices. I had not worked on a film where that was so necessary, and I learned a lot. The [practical] shooting went really well."

"When creating Alita from Rosa's performance, we pay special attention to her eyes and mouth, especially when she is speaking," Letteri says. "The facial model built for Alita had nearly 2,500 facial action shapes – three

times the number used for the groundbreaking work on Neytiri. This gave animators more precise control over the movement that creates her expressions than previously possible. We did extensive work integrating specific muscle information and tissue data to validate the proper placement of her digital skull relative to the surrounding structures. This type of precision gave us more refined expressions and fine-tuning of the micro-movements around her mouth and eyes."

"On *Alita*," Landau says, "we have really refined the science of the facial performance capture to a level that Weta has never done before. We're doing it in a humanoid character, in a photographic world, on Earth – that is a much higher standard to realize. Weta is using two hi-def cameras for the performance capture, and we're running a series of sessions that Weta calls 'FACS sessions,' where we put the performer inside of a very confined space, and they repeat the dialogue so that we get all of the nuances of their performance with not just these two cameras, but a multitude of cameras that help us to be more authentic to the actor's performance.

"From an acting standpoint," Landau continues, "doing performance capture is no different than doing live-action. We need the actors to give us all the subtleties and the nuances of their performance. We then work with Weta to bring that performance to the screen. We shoot a tremendous amount of reference of the performance, so not just the cameras that are recording the face, but off-board reference cameras. Those reference cameras stay with the shot throughout all of the post-production visual effects process. It gives us a continual reference to the performance that the actor gave on the set. We line up daily every shot that we get back from Weta, whether it be at an animation level or a lighting level, and we compare picture and picture – what did Rosa do, what did Jackie Earle Haley do, what are the characters doing?"

"One thing that helps Alita truly transcend other CG characters is her interactions with the rest of her world," Saindon points out. "We were encouraged by Robert Rodriguez and Jon Landau to allow Rosa to interact with and touch the other actors as much as possible. This adds a whole other level of integration, especially in a native 3D format, but it's quite difficult to remove the actor from the plate, so it is often avoided. Rather than shy away, we doubled down by building CG versions of all the actors in the film and tracked 3D movement so that we could always be sure Alita fit in the correct 3D space and we got the correct collisions with her hair, clothing and other characters.

"To ensure we always had the camera coverage we needed on the different sets and locations," Saindon continues, "the Weta crew would go in a few days in advance and wire up fifty to sixty cameras pointing to every part of a film set. This meant, wherever Rosa was, we would always have multiple cameras to use to calculate her movement. As added support, we had six manually operated reference cameras on Rosa at all times. Depending on the scene, these would focus on different elements. In a dialogue moment, the extra cameras would be tight on Rosa's face. In an action scene, they would be set wider to capture more angles that would help us when we were working out her movements and the interaction points with the plate elements."

While capturing the face is essential, even more is required. "You need to get the upper body and some of the movement," Hollander explains. "Even if you're just doing a talking head, you still have to capture the body to get it really going. Because Weta has been doing this so long, when it gets down to movement, they know that the concept work [prior to animation] will never address that. You get these concepts [for the] face, and some side angles and so on, and it's not what it's [ultimately] going to be; it's a suggestion. So that step is a huge step

**ABOVE:** Final still of Alita wet.

once you build in CG. A lot of conceptual artists now do the concepts based in 3D geometry, so when they rotate it, at least the proportions are the same. But before, they used to draw it and the proportions would change as they drew it, because they couldn't get it exactly right. We're getting better that way to close that gap. But even then, when they paint lighting on, you have to make that jump early and then do your design in a repeatable environment. You have to re-render it [multiple times]."

Alita has several bodies during the course of the film: Cybergirl, Berserker, and Motorballer. "Each of these bodies had a different movement style, and therefore meant a different way of thinking about Rosa's performance," Letteri says, describing the process. "When creating Alita's body, we knew developing a visual language of mannerisms and posture based on Rosa's movements was essential to maintaining Alita's character as she changed physical form throughout the film. Her Cybergirl body alone had 7,700 pieces, including her intricate mechanical internal elements and clothing. Alita's Cybergirl body is made from distinct material types comprised of different metals and featuring an alabaster skin with unique light scattering properties. Despite this mix of materials, we always made sure that each of Alita's bodies could move fluidly to capture the gracefulness of Rosa's performance. As Alita starts to connect with her former life, we see her start to own her own body as she rediscovers her knowledge of her unique cyborg fighting style, Panzer-Kunst."

When Alita decides to compete in the lethal Motorball game, Letteri says, "Animators added fast and fluid acrobatic movements that demonstrated the strength and training that builds her confidence. In her Motorball form, Alita's movements were animated to look effortless; she is clearly in her element."

However, these were simply initial stages in fully realizing Alita. "Establishing the design and movement of Alita was just the first step to bringing her into the world of the film," Letteri continues. "Her hair and clothes, as well as the different materials of her body and her skin, all played vital roles in establishing her believability. There were over 150 different hair grooms and clothing items created for Alita to fully realize her different incarnations and style variations. All of these forms had specific versions for dry, underwater, transitioning out of the water, ambient wind, motorbike speed, and Motorballer action. These were all managed with carefully art-directed simulations."

In terms of new programming, Letteri explains, "We were able to take full advantage of our new Physlight addition to our proprietary renderer, Manuka, which allowed us to add an even greater level of photographic realism to Alita. This can be seen most clearly in her skin. Being a teenage woman, she doesn't have many wrinkles or blemishes that help convey the natural properties of skin. But the subsurface scattering of light in Alita's skin, combined with a true spectral response from the renderer, gave us the ability to create a future-tech synthetic skin that still allows audiences to connect to her as fundamentally human."

Hollander points out that, as the Alita character is a Total Replacement cyborg, "That face is not real skin, but it emulates real skin. So you start to feel comfortable watching her. And she's an advanced TR, as well. I think that is the factor where, if this works, all of a sudden you forget that she's got the alabaster body, gears on the inside, or the Berserker body that's got this other, unknown technology underneath it. You should just be focusing on that performance and her issues in the movie."

There are other significant characters besides the main protagonist in *Alita* who are completely or substantially realized in CG. These include Jackie Earle Haley's tormented hulking former Motorballer Grewishka and Ed Skrein's arrogant Hunter Warrior Zapan. They went through the same design process as would fully live-action characters.

"Oftentimes, people get confused when they're dealing with something that's computer-generated," Landau says. "We had an incredible team of artists who worked to design Alita, Grewishka, Zapan, all of these characters. We would then look at the final designs we had, and we then had to determine how we were going to realize them. Just like we did when we were making *Titanic*. We knew we needed the ship, but we had to work out how much of the ship we needed to build practically and how much we could do digitally."

Landau delineates what was needed. "With Zapan, we said, 'We're going to use Ed Skrein's whole face photographically.' But Zapan's body is a computer-generated body that replaces Ed Skrein's physical body. Jackie Earle Haley, who plays Grewishka, is this powerhouse of an actor in a small frame and here he is [giving] a powerhouse performance in a very large character. As with Alita, we need to use computer-

**ABOVE & BELOW:** Filmed still of Alita and Zapan (Ed Skrein) and a final still from the same scene.
**OPPOSITE:** Filmed still from the scene with Grewishka (Jackie Earle Haley) in the surgical frame in Chiren's lab, with Vector (Mahershala Ali).

generated technology to create his performance on screen, and we do that with performance capture. We don't call it motion capture, because we don't just want the motion of a character, we want the *emotion* of a character – and that is the performance we get. That's what we do by simultaneously capturing the facial performance through a head rig that is worn by the actor and through body markers."

In the case of the gigantic Grewishka, Landau continues, "One of the unique challenges was his height. We needed to give actors the eye-line, where to look when he was on the set, so that they would know where they were reacting to. For that, we found a stuntman and put him on stilts so that he could be at the right eye level. He would walk the performance; Jackie Earle Haley would be right there giving the vocal performance and the other hand gestures that the stunt person effectively mimicked. The head height gave us the right eye-line for all the other actors in the scenes."

Hollander recalls another on-set solution. "A good, simple example is shooting the scene in Chiren's lab when Grewishka's in Chiren's repair rig. We built a chair for Jackie that he had to crawl up on, that put him up high, so his head was where Grewishka's head was going to be. So, there he sits, and his eye-line down to Jennifer Connelly is perfect."

A difference in size between performance-capture actors and the characters they're playing is not uncommon. "Any time you have a CG character, it's almost harder when you don't have the actual thing in its actual size [on set]," Hollander explains. "That changes your production quite a bit. Grewishka has three different phases. He goes from eight feet to nine feet tall. His size is enough to cause lots of problems. You want people's eye-lines in the right place." So, in order to help the live-action performers react properly, "We built a big picture of him, from the artwork, full size. And everybody said, 'Oh, I get it.' That stuff helps. For Grewishka, there's a lot of stand-and-talk, so it wasn't so hard to do. When he moves around, most of the time

**ABOVE:** Final still of Alita fighting Grewishka.

**OPPOSITE:** Preparing to film a completely CGI Motorball scene with Gangsta (Patrick Gathron), Mace (Anthony Bandmann), Alita, Stinger (Sam Medina), and Kumaza (Alan Nguyen).

he's fighting Alita, and that's all in CG."

A process called Simulcam was also beneficial. "Simulcam – meaning simultaneously capture – via a gaming engine and pipeline, generates an image that looks like Grewishka, and animates in real time, and mixes it in with the frames that are coming off the camera [into the Video Village monitors]," Hollander says. "Weta had the ability to take the performance

capture of Jackie – not his face, just his body and head movement – and put that into our model of Grewishka, in real time, where we're shooting, and composite that image of the Grewishka character back into the camera's view. So, the camera moves around and there's Grewishka, right there. On the set, there is a monitor that is the result of the camera taking [the live-action footage] and the Grewishka CG being generated live.

We did that almost every time we saw Grewishka in the film. We fed the Simulcam image back to the camera operator, so he knew where Grewishka was, how much he had grown."

Hollander gives an example of how Simulcam helped during shooting. "There's a scene where Grewishka walks into Vector's office. [Five-and-a-half-feet-tall] Jackie was walking across the floor, so Jackie's head was nowhere near where eight-or-nine-feet-tall Grewishka's head would be. [Cinematographer] Bill Pope and his team pointed the camera relative to the Simulcam view, not to where Jackie was. Now we've got Grewishka's head in the right place in the upper portion."

Even a few years back, Hollander observes, it would not have been possible to make *Alita* as it is being done now. "We've had different incarnations of the technology and it only improves. I shot pickups for crowd references using a new technology called N-Cam. Lightstorm owns one and Weta owns one. It's a wonderful way to understand where the camera is moving in 3D space. So, I had crowds I could match up to the CG shots we had already built."

For all of *Alita*'s groundbreaking CGI advances, Landau wants people to remember that it is primarily a live-action movie. "We have certain scenes that are completely computer-generated. But at the heart of it, we went out and built a 97,000-square-foot set in Austin, Texas," Landau emphasizes. "We had our actors walking on real streets interacting with each other, interacting with the environment they are on.

"If we're on a virtual stage, like we are with *Avatar*, you can set up a permanent facility within which you can do all of your capture," Landau continues. "On *Alita*, for the majority of the shoot, we were going from one physical set to another and to another. The team at Weta Digital had to come in and put up performance capture cameras all around these live-action sets in a way that they could capture the performances, but not be overtly seen in the scenes. Big challenge."

For the live-action, Landau notes, "We approached it as a very efficient production in Austin, where we had Bill Pope, the cinematographer from *The Matrix*, as our director of photography. We had Garrett Warren, our stunt coordinator from *Avatar*, and other movies like *Logan*, working with us, and treated it really like a live-action film that, in the center, had this very unique challenge of taking Rosa Salazar's performance out of photography and creating her character through computer-generated imagery."

All of the technical elements also had to serve the distinctive vision and style of director Robert Rodriguez. "We're accommodating Robert's fast and furious style of shooting as much as we can," says Hollander. "He's got his own style of making decisions and coming to conclusions and asking for different things. Weta did a lot of design work so they could do similar things to their work on *Apes*. They had a large crew on set at all times, large amounts of equipment, cameras by every single set, performance capture cameras being moved around all the time, because we almost always had a performance by Rosa. We wanted to make that whole environment as seamless as possible for Robert. It was pretty amazing."

"There are certain action sequences that are all virtual," Landau adds, "and for those sequences, we turned to the process that we used on *Avatar*, which I call virtual production. When an actor goes onto a performance [capture] stage, we have a performance capture system and a virtual camera, and we realize the sequences virtually."

Integrating CGI into a live-action shot and creating a completely CG shot for a film that is largely live-action both present challenges. "Implementing anything CG in a live-action frame in 3D is challenging because there's an integration issue between the two," explains Hollander. "This film was shot in native 3D with two cameras. When you try to integrate things that aren't real with everything else, it adds a whole other dimension in energy and technical expertise. But on the other hand, the challenge with an all-CG scene is to make it look like it's not CG. Today, it's easier than it was five years ago, with better tools for rendering, but you have to work at it and the difficulty level depends on the environment that you're trying to duplicate."

Of the work Lightstorm and Weta are doing together on *Alita*, Landau concludes, "We have been working with Weta for more than ten years now, and we have a great shorthand to get through this process. We have a team of people here [at Lightstorm's headquarters in Southern California]. They work daily, hours upon hours, with Weta. It would not be unusual for us to have six-, seven-hour reviews with Weta looking at these shots on a frame-by-frame basis. The relationship with Weta is, first, a friendship, and second, this incredibly rewarding collaboration."

# DYSON IDO

Dr. Dyson Ido is a man conflicted. By day he is a cyber-physician who repairs cyborgs and at night, a crime-stopping Hunter-Warrior who kills rogue cyborgs. Despite this intriguing dichotomy, James Cameron says a different factor attracted Oscar®-winning actor Christoph Waltz to the character. As with Cameron himself and director Robert Rodriguez, Waltz was moved by the relationship between Ido and his adopted cyborg daughter Alita. "At first Christoph was a little lukewarm," Cameron recalls. "I said, 'Do you have kids?' He said, 'Yeah, I have a daughter.' I said, 'Well, this is about fathers and daughters. Yes, it's a [romantic] love story, but it's also a love story on another axis, which is the father coming to terms with the daughter's independence.' Once he saw his way into it as a father, he got excited about doing the film."

Character designer Joe Pepe began work on Ido before Waltz was cast. Ido's jacket, hat and glasses were all taken from the original manga art. "Everything I do, I start with what was there in the original art, and I elaborate on that, and make it photo-realistic," Pepe says. "I scuffed up the jacket a bit more, I put cuts and tears in it, trying to think about the environment that he's been in, and how beat up and abused his tools and wardrobe are, based on his location."

Costume designer Nina Proctor notes that Ido has different looks and types of coats for his different personas. "Nothing too futuristic, though." Repairing cyborgs requires cyborg parts, which means Ido often starts his day scavenging in the Scrapyard. The coat Ido wears while doing this "was not quite full-length. We custom-made it in our shop here in Austin, but I chose

**BELOW & OPPOSITE:** Concept art of Ido in Iron City.
**BELOW RIGHT:** Photo of Ido's binoculars

**RIGHT:** Ido (Christoph Waltz) dressed for his cybersurgeon work.

a linen, and then we did a wax treatment over it. It did have areas that had leather, but because we waxed the linen, it almost had a leather look to it, but it wasn't heavy like leather. It gave it great movement. That coat is warmer [to wear], and it's warmer in color, not as dark as the Hunter-Warrior coat." Its thickness, Proctor observes, protects Ido from being cut by the Scrapyard metal. He wears gloves for much the same reason. "Those were a pair of old vintage army gloves, so they looked practical for digging around."

Like its scavenging counterpart, the Hunter-Warrior coat also offers Ido protection from cyborg parts, though these belong to live cyborgs who are trying to kill him. Ido's Hunter-Warrior look, Proctor elaborates, "was a harder, a darker look, and it was all leather. Most of that was shot at night, and in the winter, so we were grateful for that. And it goes through quite a bit of damage throughout the film."

How does a dark coat remain visible in night sequences? "I never just go with one solid dark [shade]," Proctor explains. "There's a lot of aging involved. He's seen many battles in this coat by the time our movie starts. I chose a dark-to-medium brown leather, and then did a lot of processes where I took some of that color back out of the leather. And there were different textures in the leather. It had a lot of slashes and cuts and damage, and then it would be mended. And as the movie progressed, he gets hurt several times, so there were new mends on it."

**LEFT & ABOVE:** Ido dressed for his cybersurgeon work.

Proctor took pains so that the coats did not closely resemble any that Waltz had worn in previous films. "Christoph Waltz was awesome to work with. I did a lot of research once he was cast. He has done some films where he was in long, full-length coats, and I didn't want it to look just like any other coat that he'd ever worn. I was keeping my fingers crossed that he liked the choices that I made. He was very happy."

Proctor decided early in the development process that today's folded shirt collars wouldn't do for any of the denizens of Iron City, including Ido. "I tried to just do away with collars, because that's something that we [in the present] do to enhance the way something looks. It's a vanity thing. So Ido has a lot of collar-band shirts."

Then there's Ido's hat, which Proctor physically pummeled with a rubber hammer. "I'm very hands-on as a costume designer," she laughs. "For something like Dr. Ido's hat, I have to be the one working it with my hands. I pound on it. I work it just by pulling and stretching on the leather. There are different conditioners that you can use. There is sanding that happens to it. Once I get the hat to a point where I'm feeling good about the weight, the shape and the look of it, there are a lot of products for antiquing leather, and that's where you get more depth. Each thing you do to it gives it a little bit more depth and a little bit more presence. I like things to look like they belong to a person, in this case that it had been Ido's hat for a long time."

Proctor says that Ido's glasses are technically considered props rather than part of the wardrobe department. "Although when I'm doing the fitting, if an actor is going to be wearing glasses, or accessories like rings or watches, I set a table outside my fitting room, and let the prop people come in and lay their props out. I have mirrors that go all the way across my fitting room wall. So the first time [the actor] gets into costume we're able to try the glasses and the coat and the hat on all together. Robert [Rodriguez] loves to be there, especially for those things, because it's an object on the face, it's so much part of the character."

**LEFT:** Photo of Ido's Hunter-Warrior ID badge.
**ABOVE:** Concept art of Ido collecting a Hunter-Warrior bounty.
**RIGHT:** Costume design for Ido's Hunter-Warrior clothing.

**ABOVE & OPPOSITE:** Ido with his rocket hammer on a Hunter-Warrior job.
**RIGHT:** 3D prop models for the rocket hammer and case.

# IDO'S ROCKET HAMMER

For Ido's Hunter-Warrior work, his weapon of choice is his rocket hammer. "Ido's rocket hammer is an iconic element of the manga," production designer Caylah Eddleblute says. "It comes in a sequence of parts. Ido needs to be able to get that thing out of its case, assemble it and fire it. When you have an actor who's really comfortable with the parts and understands them, and they work well, it makes everything so much nicer."

Alongside the rocket hammer, another key prop for Ido is the rolling suitcase where he keeps his Hunter-Warrior weaponry. "That suitcase sets up some of the mystery of Ido at the beginning," production designer Steve Joyner observes. "Alita is aware that Ido goes out at night, but she doesn't understand what he's actually doing. It turns out that he is using the rocket hammer for good, not evil."

Each hero prop used in *Alita* is designed to operate in three beats: acquisition, assembly or activation and operation. "We teach our fabrication crew to rehearse with every single prop that's designed," says Eddleblute, "so they know what's industrial strength, they know that the actors can operate in beats of three. I learned this from watching [director] Robert Rodriguez and [actor] Antonio Banderas work. That really helps the actors a lot, because then they have a good sense of rhythm in the scene."

For the case, "Our property master Jason Hammond brought in a number of samples," Eddleblute recalls. "He, our fabrication department head, Sarah King, and I worked carefully to make sure the colors and interior were just so. Sarah and her team did a beautiful

layout of all the parts inside the case, how they would come out, and they rehearsed with the parts inside the case."

"That suitcase is custom-fitted for Christoph Waltz," Joyner says. "It was based on a military case that was aluminum-shelled. We cut it down a little bit, and we put universal casters on the bottom, so we could roll it upright, like a four-wheeled luggage cart, and the interior, in keeping with Ido's warm theme, is form-fitted, almost like an assassin's rifle case, where all the parts are laid out in pockets. Except we did it with deerskin leather, so it has that rich, careworn feel of Ido, to differentiate it from the cold weapons that

the jackers are using. Also, we knew the case couldn't overpower Christoph when he was on the road, so we designed the rocket hammer where it just assembles, so that no piece was longer than the case was tall. It would comfortably ride just below his waist."

The rocket hammer is also a practical physical prop, Joyner reveals. "One of our 3D artists here at Troublemaker, Alex Toader, has a 3D printer in his office, so we were able to set parts as they were being designed. He's very good at doing three-dimensional assemblies. We put a practical mockup in Robert's hand early on, and he gave us notes off that. You see all the working parts to it, and it fires in cartridges. The cartridges are built, the shapers are built, and you really physically understand the working of it."

There are several versions of the rocket hammer. "We had complete, hundred-percent photo-real disassembled versions that Christoph could snap together that are a little bit heavier," Joyner says. "We have a version made out of aluminum and very lightweight parts for fighting. The fabrication shop took a mold of the completed version and then made rubber parts for the stunt version and fit them either over a real handle or the end of it would be rubber. They made several versions with different soft parts on it, so he could hit things with it and not hurt the other actors."

The rocket hammer prop actually dictated the size of a set. "Ido needed enough room to swing this hammer. We designed Ambush Alley [where Ido fights Nyssiana and Romo] with that in mind," explains art director A. Todd Holland. "We'd come up with the concepts, built the model, gave it to pre-vis, they ran their action through it, and we needed more space. So we made some slight adjustments, and the final version of that alleyway was just big enough to make a good swing of that hammer."

**LEFT:** Ido with his rocket hammer.
**RIGHT:** Early (2005) concept art of Ido with his rocket hammer.

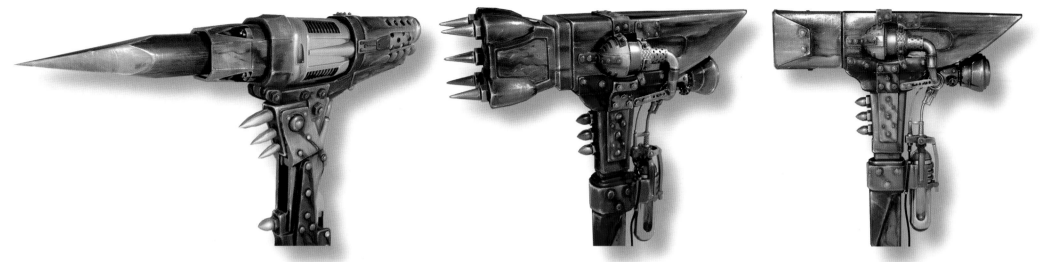

**ABOVE & BELOW:** 3D concept designs of the rocket hammer.

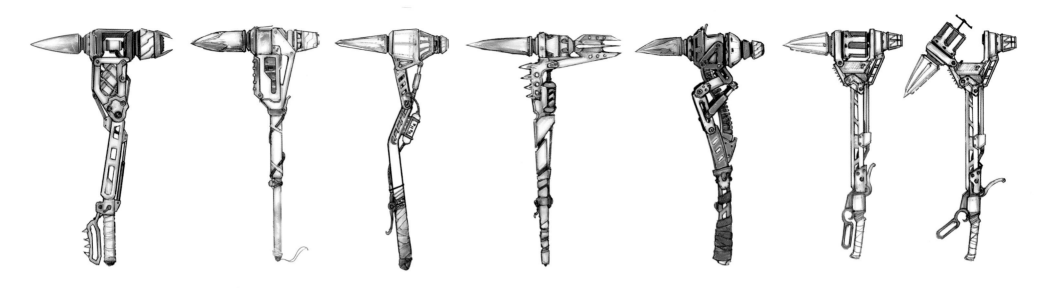

**ABOVE:** Concept designs for the rocket hammer.
**BELOW:** Early (2005) concept art of Ido wielding the rocket hammer in his Hunter-Warrior work.

# IDO'S DAUGHTER

We only see Dyson Ido and Chiren's daughter, the human Alita Ido, in flashback. The wheelchair-bound girl is murdered by a junkie cyborg looking for drugs in Ido's clinic. Her death leads to her parents' split, but it gives new life to the cyborg Alita when Ido uses the delicate filigreed cyborg body he had made for his own child to house the active female cyber core he finds in the Scrapyard.

In the story, "Ido made the wheelchair with love, for his daughter," production designer Caylah Eddleblute says. "So you see how it's different and the care and love that he put into it." She notes that fellow production designer Steve Joyner cut the inset pieces for the chair, using CNC, a system whereby a computer controls the manufacturing tools.

Costume designer Nina Proctor says that, for Cybergirl Alita, "I wanted it to be like Ido used his daughter's stored clothes, so we tried to dress [the biological daughter] in the same fashions for the flashbacks. We did a little pair of jeans and a similar pair of shoes to those Alita wears at the beginning of the movie, a little high-top tennis shoe and a simple top. But because he had preserved his daughter's bedroom, and that was Cybergirl Alita's bedroom, I wanted it to indicate that's where he came up with the clothing to dress Alita."

Cybergirl Alita is given Alita Ido's bedroom. "[Set decorator] Dave Hack worked on that for a long time," Joyner says. "Her room was designed to be a grieving parent's preservation of the memory of their child, containing everything that was given to her and that she treasured. So all the objects in her room were selected to show the love that Ido and Chiren had for her, that ghost of a memory."

There's even a teddy bear. "We presented Robert with three teddy bears," Joyner recalls, "and Robert turned to Rosa [Salazar], our actress playing Alita, and said, 'What would you have?' And Rosa picked one without even hesitating. So the final decision was made by Rosa."

**LEFT:** Photo of Alita Ido's wheelchair.
**ABOVE:** Alita Ido's bedroom set.

# IDO'S CLINIC

Ido's clinic was one of the first sets completed. "We prioritized sets like Ido's building and his operating room, because we had to shoot there and there wasn't going to be any digital adding onto it," director Robert Rodriguez explains. "It needed to be completely nailed down."

"The set was quite big," art director A. Todd Holland recalls. "We changed it around and worked on it for a long time." For the exterior, "We found interesting images from Cuba. One day I was in Austin, looking through one of Steve Joyner's reference books. I landed on a page and, seeing the image, I said, 'That is Ido's.' [Production designers] Steve [Joyner] and Caylah [Eddleblute] agreed. We loved it."

**BELOW & RIGHT:** Concept art of the clinic operating room.
**ABOVE:** Photo of an operating room robotic arm.

**ABOVE:** Concept art of the operating table.

It turns out they weren't the only ones. Holland says that later, when looking through Lightstorm's massive collection of reference photos and concept art for *Alita* dating back to 2005, "I found an image of the very same building in Cuba. It had been reversed, but they'd done a little sketch of it with Ido, back in 2005. So, that they saw that and felt that then, and we saw it again in 2015 and felt the same, it seemed like we were moving in the right direction."

For the practical interior location, "Steve and Caylah picked out this flatiron-exterior building that we found,"

Holland continues, "and this interior could fit into that world. It had wonderful arches, and an old-school grand feeling. We thought it [had been] either a casino or an old bank building, with a nice ornate lobby, but also some locked areas – not steel cages, but where the cashiers are. It's a little more protected. Where the bank tellers were, that's where we had Hugo's recovery room in the infirmary. It had these great doors everywhere, which we would use on the exterior lot as well, with this wonderful spot for some stained glass, which was going to be the tie-in between the exterior back lot and the

interior set."

The doors were manufactured by the *Alita* construction department, "Because we needed so many, and they're all identical," Holland explains. "It's very hard to find that many in architectural salvage. I needed twelve double doors. The stained glass I needed to also do on the back lot and on the interiors. So to have control of that, we designed and completely manufactured that in-house."

The interior set had to be large enough to accommodate everything, Eddleblute says, including

**ABOVE:** The clinic set, including the operating table.

the camera crane. It had numerous sections: "Intimate settings from Ido's life when he lived with Chiren, his office area, he's got his kitchen area, he's got his lab. The interior setting has such grandeur to it, and history."

"When you read the script and you look at the concept art, there were seven or eight different environments there," Joyner relates. "Our idea was to set up everything in this grand room, so that the surgery, where he repairs cyborgs, is always in the background, when he's in the kitchen or his living room or at his desk doing research. Caylah and I always try to create an interesting space with a lot of sets. We also break it down by [script] page count. Ido's has the highest page count of the environments in the movie. 'Hey, we're spending a lot of time here, let's do something big and memorable in this space.'"

Ido's operating theatre "was a collaborative affair between props, set dressing and the art department," Holland says. "We found this great table that we liked, and one of our set designers reworked that, redesigned it, made it a little more fanciful."

"We modified that with monitors and displays," Joyner continues, "and lit it with internal LEDs. It has a collage effect to it. Whereas Chiren's equipment we did build with a CNC [computer numerical control] machine and her stuff is all very similar; 180 degrees opposite of Ido's clinched-together lab. Ido's equipment is salvaged and

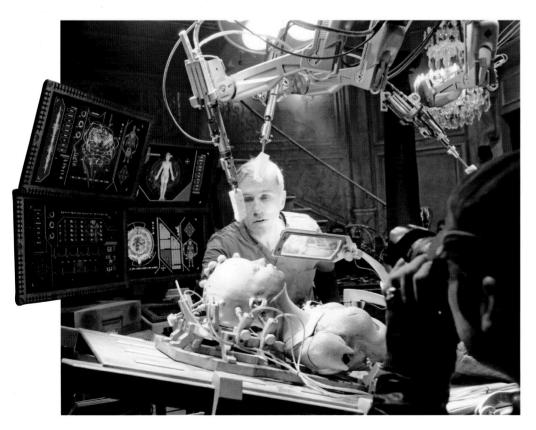

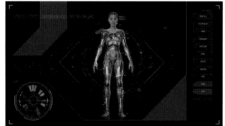

**LEFT:** Behind the scenes photo of filming Ido preparing to place Alita's cyber core into the doll body.
**ABOVE:** Operating room display graphics of Alita.
**RIGHT:** Ido's hand-drawn annotated schematic of a cyborg arm.

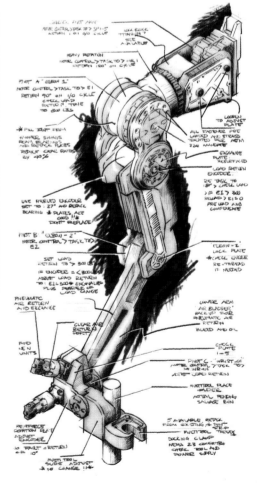

**ABOVE:** Concept art of Ido checking Alita's doll body for damage.
**ABOVE RIGHT:** Final still of Ido checking Alita's doll body for damage.

much more organic, and Ido modifies it."

There is also a frame in Ido's operating room where he works on his cyborg patients. "The frame was built from a collection of walkways that they used to service B-52 [plane]s back in the day," Joyner reveals.

The operating room has robotic arms that assist Ido and Nurse Gerhad with their surgeries. "There had been a number of different studies over the years, some from 2005, some from 2016," Holland says. "I think one of our in-house illustrators, Shane Baxley, did the final pass of the arms. Paul Alix, our assistant art director, developed it even further, using a lot of found pieces that Steve, Paul and I found in some other architectural salvage places, and incorporating them all together. Austin is a treasure trove of aircraft salvage and technology. So we would spend a couple days, go to these places [the size of] multiple football fields, and find great aluminum extrusions, glasswork that you just normally wouldn't see, anything you could have. Steve, Paul and I would make piles, and then bid on it, buy it, and work within the set. Iron City is a salvage society. Why wouldn't they use those kinds of things?"

Like the rest of the Ido set, the robot arms were practical, at least when they weren't moving. "They look like dental tools or the lights

**LEFT:** Early (2005) concept art of Alita in her doll body waking up in Ido's daughter's bedroom.

above your head in a dentist's office," Holland says. "They're on swing arms with multiple joints so they can get to different avenues, and each has a different set of tools. Some look sharp, some look more like screwdrivers, some look more like pincers or wrenches or whatever is necessary for the type of cyborg surgery that's needed."

"They cannot move automatically," Holland clarifies, "but they are fully poseable. We didn't want them to actually move practically anyway, because VFX wanted them to move very fast and wanted to be in control of that. So we could put them up and pose them in the space we wanted when they're static, but also easily remove them at the joint so VFX can redo them and take them over when they're moving and functioning."

Ido's surgical optical rig differs from the one he uses in the manga. "The optical rig in the book is worn on the face, and I didn't want to mess with Christoph's face at all," Joyner says. "My solution to that was to build the optical rig into his operating table, so it is on an arm that he can look through and see what he needs to see, and that leaves his face clear to emote and act."

To help convey Ido's warmth visually, Eddleblute reveals, "His environment has more rounded edges. The exterior of his building even has architectural details, rounded balconies, echoing his personality in a setting that isn't quite so hard-edged, and with a beautiful staircase that has rounded [curves]."

In Ido's living area, "You could feel the history of his previous life with Chiren," Eddleblute says. "There were living areas that were set up, and then as time went on, you can feel the segue as his work took over the environment."

"The décor was meant to be very eclectic," Joyner explains. "Set decorator David Hack and his team started with a real sense of order and décor in what would have been the living room, with nice furniture, nice lamp, nice table, things that would have been chosen with care by a couple. One half of that couple is now gone, and the other half of the couple has taken that over and covered it with machine parts and bits and pieces of his current world. He definitely misses Chiren. There's a melancholy to it."

"Christoph Waltz gave us one of the nicest compliments that I've ever received," Joyner recalls of a happy moment related to the set. "After working in the interior space that we created for him, he turned to me and said, 'I've never been on a set where so much stuff is practical.' Apparently it really made him feel the character."

**LEFT:** Concept art of patients waiting to see Ido at the clinic.
**ABOVE:** One of Ido's patients (John Wirt).

# NURSE GERHAD

Ido's assistant, Nurse Gerhad, is distinguished by her cyber arm, which contains all sorts of useful surgical implements. Consequently, actress Idara Victor spent the film with a grey "sock" over her real left arm. "Her arm is completely digitally generated," explains Weta senior visual effects supervisor Joe Letteri, "because it has to articulate. As she's preparing for surgery, the tools unfold and get themselves ready."

"It's basically her medical toolkit," elaborates Weta visual effects supervisor Eric Saindon. "We tried to cram as many medical tools as we could into her arm – lasers, scalpels, some syringes – and we put them all on little moving rigs, so that in different scenes, she can use different parts within her arm to do as many medical things as possible, which means always having her arm doing something, moving around, giving it a life of its own." That way Gerhad never has to reach for any tools. "They all just come out as they need to."

Character designer Joe Pepe began working on Gerhad with "some initial key frames where her robotic arm is working on Alita's cyber core. Several cybernetic versions were taken from earlier versions, the 2005 artwork I believe [lead concept artist] Mark Goerner had done, and then it was slightly modified to [visual consultant] Ben [Procter]'s taste. Ben and I had worked on some street clothes for her, and then also her surgical arm and street arm." For Gerhad's outside-the-office look, "We figured she had a favorite Motorballer and picked one. We put her in a Kinuba shirt. Ben wanted to make something that was a little more futuristic and sporty, so it was a combination of me playing around, and then him coming in and art-directing it until we got something we thought was fun."

"The shirt was like a football jersey," says costume designer Nina Proctor. "I made her this cool piece that she wore over the shirt that was made out of a neoprene, almost scuba suit fabric, but variegated in color, so it's all these shades of blue. It did look a little more futuristic than some of the other pieces, but it fit her personality. I believe she wore leggings and ankle boots with it."

There were special costume requirements because of Gerhad's cybernetic arm. Every cyborg body part has a "delineator," where machinery meets flesh. "If you had a cyborg arm, you would have to have a way that it connected to your body," Proctor continues. "So we reshaped the shoulder a little bit. I made a piece that she wore on her shoulder to build up that left shoulder. It was sculpted, [made] out of a dense foam that can be cut and shaped, not like a soft shoulder pad foam." The shoulder piece is present even when the cyber arm is covered by a sleeve. "All her costumes were designed around the delineator. We were really focusing on her arm, so I sculpted that [shoulder piece] out to her own shoulder, so it fit and moved with her arm."

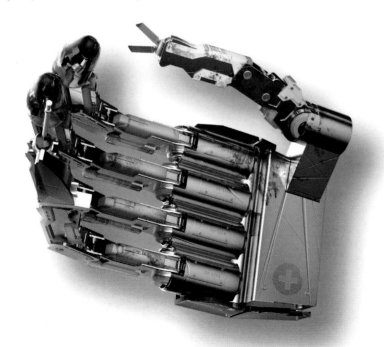

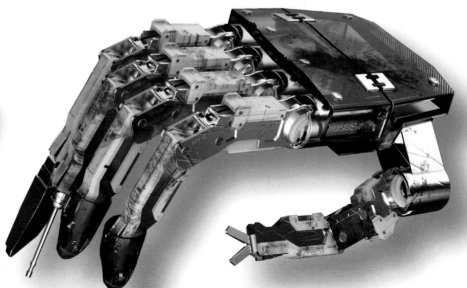

**ABOVE:** 3D concept designs of Gerhad's surgical cyber hand.

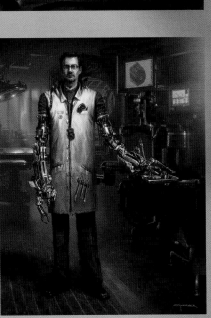

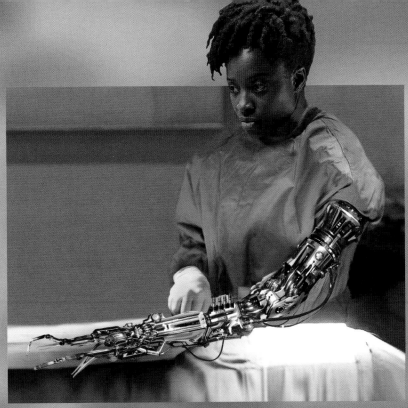

**THIS PAGE (EXCEPT RIGHT):** Concept art of Gerhad and the surgical cyber arm.
**RIGHT:** Idara Victor as Gerhad dressed for her cybernurse work.

# IDO'S PATIENTS

Ido's patients dress pretty much like everybody else in Iron City – that is, each one has an individual style. "We have a Factory worker, and of course he is very dirty, greasy," says costume designer Nina Proctor, giving an eample. "He pays the doctor with a bag of oranges. When I dress the background [extras], they send forty people at a time [for] fittings, but you really have to look at each person. You don't just randomly dress them; you have to study your script, and know where these background people are working."

One of Dr. Ido's patients is a "jacked" cyborg who has had his limbs stolen. Weta visual effects supervisor Eric Saindon explains how they achieved the visuals. "We took the actor on set, we stuck his legs inside the table, and then he held his arms behind him. We're taking out his arms and legs and adding CG stumps, so he's basically just a torso."

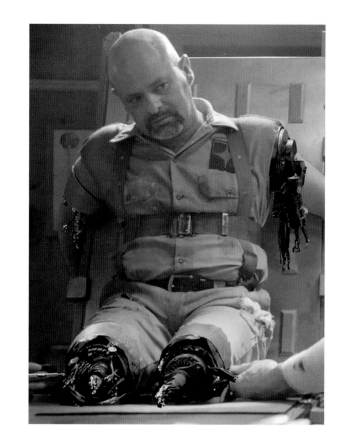

**CLOCKWISE FROM ABOVE:** A patient who has been "jacked" (Hugo Perez); Concept art of the patient before the jacking; Concept art of Ido with the patient.

# AMOK CYBORG

We see in flashback the pivotal incident when a cyborg runs amok in Ido's clinic and kills Ido's young daughter. This breaks up Ido and Chiren's relationship and inspires Ido to become a Hunter-Warrior, then later to repair and adopt "Cybergirl" Alita.

For the physical aspect of the "Amok Cyborg," Weta visual effects supervisor Eric Saindon says, "We [digitally] replaced the actor's torso. We used a live-action head, and we're using live-action waist down, and then we're giving him a bigger torso, a more muscular cyber-body, with one missing arm and big over-the-top upper arms, because he is an ex-Motorball player."

The cyborg is dressed somewhat like a junkie, costume designer Nina Proctor explains. "He broke into Ido's clinic to steal drugs. He's a very rough character, some really aged, dirty, hole-y jeans. We always try to be conscious of the footwear. I had him in a heavy-duty boot, and then the sleeves were ripped out of his shirt, so the raw edges of the shirt were visible."

**THIS PAGE:** Concept art of the cyborg.

# IRON CITY

"In our film, it's centuries after a huge war has devastated the planet," James Cameron says of the setting for *Alita: Battle Angel*. "Only a tiny percentage of humanity survived. The survivors formed a giant refugee camp in the shadow of Zalem, the Sky City that floats a mile or so above them. They can never get there, because Zalem had severed the connection to the ground."

Over the centuries since the war, the survivor encampment on Earth became Iron City. "One of the core principles of the story is, when Zalem was connected [to the planet's surface], it was connected by a space elevator," producer Jon Landau explains. "Science-wise, for a space elevator to exist, it needs to be on or near the equator. We're doing things that are science-fact, not just science-fiction. So we're going to ground it in a South American city. Iron City, over centuries, has one layer of development built upon another and another. You look at what once existed, and then different layers were built using different technologies."

Landau adds that most of Iron City's residents don't see their lives as post-apocalyptic. "While some of them might aspire to go to Zalem, this is their home and they're living there happily."

Like most aspects of *Alita*, Iron City was first born in the original manga (with a different name) and then developed in the film's concept art. A great deal of work was done in 2005, when Cameron first contemplated making *Alita*. When Robert Rodriguez came aboard to direct, new concept artists used the earlier material as reference for imagery that was then used by both physical production design and the CG artists as a basis going forward.

"The city is a highly dense architectural statement," concept artist Steve Messing says. "People are stacked in these jumbled layers of living quarters. We looked at a lot of references from photo books of Kowloon's walled city, which was demolished in 1993. A lot of the development work I did was shots up in the city streets, layering in the culture and the set dressing, blending in these different flavors of architecture. A lot of that was initial concept design work, but then it turned into later production art, after we had built some sets. We had that iconic triangular-shaped building that [production physically] built two stories of. And then we'd take spherical 360-degree photos on set. Because I have a lot of matte painting experience for visual effects, I was one of the people who took those photos. We stitched them together in a sphere, and I would do layouts of what the digital extensions would look like as a concept. We could then have a virtual look around it, 360 degrees, to get a feel for what the set extensions could be."

Visual consultant Dylan Cole describes some of the initial division of responsibility in the design process. "We all cross-pollinate. Me, [fellow visual consultant] Ben Proctor and [production designer] Steve Joyner would all do rounds together. Ben is amazing at tech design and robot design, so he naturally fell into the cyborg land. I'm more of an environment guy, [but] I would chime in on the cyborg stuff, Ben would chime in on the environment, and Steve was involved in all of it."

The concept art often incorporates elements of photographs as well as painting, Messing relates. "We get a lot of great real references and try to keep the concept art fairly grounded, at a real scale of what it would be. Sometimes people fall in love with these really detailed key frames [signature images] that we do, and they want to replicate it." This is sometimes not possible, due to differences in scale. "So we always try to

**THIS IMAGE:** Concept art of an Iron City panorama, with the Motorball stadium in the background.

**THIS IMAGE:** Concept art of Alita in her Berserker body navigating the Iron City rooftops.

**ABOVE:** Concept art of the Iron City rooftops at sunset.

set things up in a 3D model, even if it's basic scale cubes that we can stack together and make a city. Then you can wrap simple textures for doorways, and say, 'Okay, that building way out there, I know the door is correct at that distance,' so I'm not way off when I'm painting."

Making a physical set for Iron City required actual real estate. Fortunately, Rodriguez has his own Troublemaker Studios in Austin, Texas. "We built

this South American city in my [studio] parking lot," Rodriguez says. "The first couple of stories look like South America of today, with some tweaks and some retrofitting. As you pan up, the digital elements take over, it gets more futuristic and piled on. It's fun to walk around that town and go, 'Oh, my God, this town looks just like the town from *El Mariachi*,'" he cites his first feature, made for $7,000, "placed into the biggest movie

I've ever done."

The enormous scope of *Alita* called for some additional soundstages to be rented from Austin Studios and other nearby facilities. Production designers Steve Joyner and Caylah Eddleblute know exactly what it took to raise Iron City: four months and six days, 7,864 man days, on a back lot approximately 61,250 square feet in size, utilizing 480,000 pounds of concrete, stucco and

work in the factory."

"James Cameron does meticulous research," art director A. Todd Holland says. "Not only did he have this treasure trove of imagery that he wanted, but he also did this bible [in which] he'd discuss in meticulous detail where he thought this city could be, based a lot on Havana, Cuba, as well as Lisbon, Portugal, and Panama City, and then introduced different new elements on top of that. We had some influences from China, as well. It's supposed to be a very international-type city. We wanted a broad spectrum of that, but colonialism is the basis of it. I traveled to Morocco, Mumbai, India, Portugal, Istanbul, Turkey, a lot of cities where it's very tight and narrow.

"I take a lot of photographs of doors and windows and alleyways when I travel," Holland adds, "and I encourage other set designers to do the same thing."

What sort of building materials would endure into the twenty-sixth century? "Obviously, steel and stone last hundreds and hundreds of years," Holland observes. "So we knew that if we used those materials as a starting place, they could still be there when we add our newer composites – plastics, LEDs – on top of that, fabrics of the new world."

Of all the structures in Iron City, the Factory is central. To emphasize this, Cole says, he made towers with crane arms to "show that it's all a larger industrial complex, to keep hinting at industry, to give a refinery look to a lot of these high-rises. I referenced a lot of interiors of factories and refineries and power plants for all these different pipe patterns, and came up with a composition and a flow that I liked, and then built the city around that." For residences with sides open to the elements, "I've used photos of under-construction buildings, [like] a deserted thing that has since been inhabited."

A balance had to be struck. "It's an industrial, smoky city, [but] you want that fun, sun-drenched Latin American street market vibe," Cole notes, "and not have it be a depressing, dark movie."

It only takes a few days for Cole to create complex, textured images. "That's the beauty of working in layers in Photoshop," he says. Various physical elements – a building, pipes, a bridge, lighting, atmosphere – can be placed on separate layers, allowing for individual alterations to each one. "Sometimes, you just have to flatten it and start painting on top of it, but I try to keep all my layers as separate as I can to allow for changes and tweaks that need to be done," Cole explains.

The concept art also had to convey how Iron City looked from above, Messing says. "We have angles coming down the [Zalem supply] tube, so what does Iron City look like from there? How much do we see? Are there clouds?"

To distinguish *Alita*'s look further, "We used steampunk-style pipes running through the city, [which create] big, dominating forms that break up the space," Messing continues. "Having the Latin influences [provided] these bold, punchy colors of paint: orange sandstone; a bold stucco wall painted intense red, but it's decaying and it's got texture to it."

Cole adds, "We tried to limit our palettes. We would mute some of the brighter colors so that a chunk of the set wouldn't stand out, like, 'Oh, my God, there's the crazy pink building!' We would try to age them down, because these things were freshly painted hundreds of years ago. There are many color variations, but it's all a little bit more muted. There are some brighter color accents, though, whether it be vehicles or clothing or set decoration elements."

"We wanted to feel the whole city was a painting," Eddleblute elaborates. "So that everything felt unified, we had relatively strong neutral [hues], and then let certain colors sing, so that the eye could travel around the environment to different focal areas. That required walking the perimeter several times a day and looking at all the buildings from different vantage points."

Rodriguez typically has warm colors in his work, Eddleblute observes, while Landau "was always saying, 'Color, color, color.' So it was really thrilling to thread that needle. One part of town [is] more neutral, another has rich layering and is multi-colored, while the slum

plaster. "And no serious injuries," Joyner adds.

Making things look right, Joyner explains, is not enough for a film produced by James Cameron. "He makes sure there's nothing in the environment that couldn't actually work. The mechanics have to be right, the physics have to be right. It's science fiction, but it's grounded in physical reality." For a production designer, "It's like being invited into Willy Wonka's and getting to

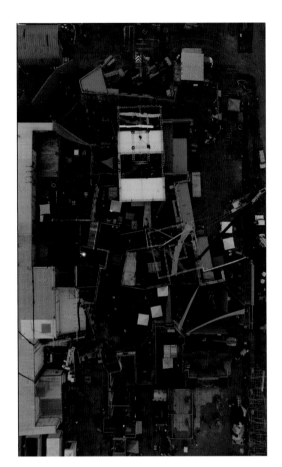

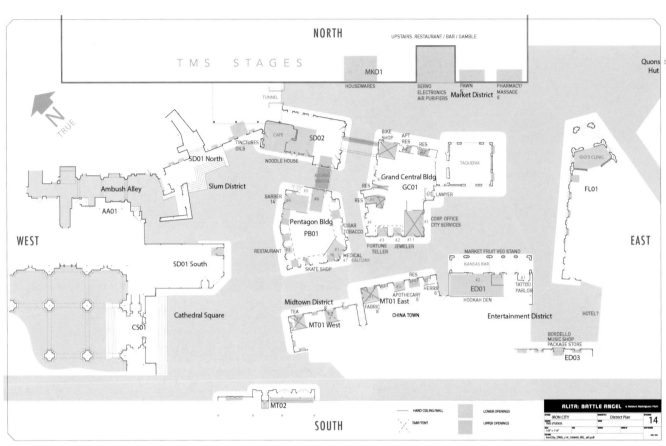

**ABOVE:** Aerial photo of a section of the Iron City streets sets under construction (left) and the District Plan for the sets (right).

district has more vibrant colors. One of the things that [cinematographer] Bill Pope was really keen on was creating buildings that had an opaque look and buildings that had almost transparent washes on them, and then the interplay of light on all those surfaces made the buildings dance in their color quality."

Joyner and Eddleblute used reference photos from places they had visited in Latin America, including Mexico City, San Miguel and Guanajuato in Mexico, and Casco Viejo in the old part of Panama City. Additionally, Eddleblute says, "There were pieces of concept art that Jim [Cameron] had keyed on, so we took those into the world we created for the overall structure of Iron City. We made a number of [computer program] InDesign pages of photo reference and tone and palette. The concept artists took that data, and were able to extrapolate out great concept art, and then we had a great team of art directors and set designers, and

they were able to then put that into our physical plans." This pleased Rodriguez, who has his own experience in these areas. "He's an artist, he's a painter, he's a sculptor," Eddleblute continues, "he's very particular about how light hits surfaces."

"Robert is also a cinematographer," Joyner points out. "Though on this film, we were fortunate enough to have Bill Pope [in that role]. We spent a lot of time with him, thinking about the textures, the colors, the depth, where we can create shadows."

The final design for Iron City can be roughly divided into three visually different areas. "We had a section in the center of town that was reminiscent of Panama City," Eddleblute says. "That was more neutral, stone colors with hints of rose. On the other side of that was the old city of stately buildings, which is where Ido's clinic is, faded glory, buildings of stature, and there was a lot of Cuban reference for that. Then we had the

section we nicknamed the slum district, which is where the kids hang out."

Holland says it was important for *Alita* to get away from neon lighting, a hallmark of '80s futuristic films. The logic being that "In two hundred years, there would be no neon left – people aren't going to be servicing it. So we used newer types of lighting applications." Joyner found industrial fixtures used in swimming pool fabrication. Most people never see the outsides of these, which means they will be novel to most viewers. "We painted them silver and then rusty iron, and the set lighting crew installed LED lights in them, and they became our high-tech street lights," explains Joyner.

Eddleblute recalls, "We had countless cranes on the back lot set and they all were rigged to hoist these massive trusses, which were rigged with spotlighting to make really dramatic light during the day and black and canvas-colored rags that would flutter in the air and create believable shadow."

The lights visible on set often also helped the camera. "It's often difficult for the DP [director of photography, or cinematographer] to pump light into cavities," Joyner says, "so we pay a lot of attention to lighting the interiors of shelves, alcoves, things that open up."

Graphic designer Ellen Lampl designed various types of signs in multiple languages for Iron City, "to show the different cultures coming together," Joyner continues, "so we tried to have as wide a range as possible. What they're trying to convey is mostly the services offered to the people. We had cyber parts and parts for sale, almost constructionism slogans like…"

"'Keep your parts clean and well-oiled,'" Eddleblute finishes. Good advice for the largely cyborg population.

A key aspect of the job "is understanding three-dimensional space and how people and cameras move through it," Eddlueblute adds. "To bring two-dimensional drawings or plans into a three-dimensional world, Steve and I will tape out our sets and literally rehearse every beat, every scene, walk through everything, so we know that the action is going to work,

that you have room for the crane, you have enough entrances and exits, wild [movable] walls, and settings that are intimate."

Some pieces of the practical set were made in Troublemaker's fabrication shop. Others were found via what Holland calls "architectural salvaging. We found different doors and windows, wrought iron, as well as aircraft parts and other things. We made a pile. You sift through it and decide, 'I want to use this piece, and that piece, use that piece,' and then you draw it into the set."

"Our set decorating department found salvaged windows," Joyner says, "salvaged iron work, things that had been removed from buildings, buying them and then redesigning our plans to incorporate them into the design. So we had these wonderful pieces that had been weathered for a hundred years and actually built them in, and then layered on that we'd have a window, and then we'd have iron work, and then we'd have some kind of added-on high-tech screen. It gives you this depth going through it, and then Bill Pope would backlight that at night."

Holland estimates there are fifteen to eighteen

buildings on the Iron City set, "depending on how you break it up. We had a five-sided building – we called it the Pentagon for shorthand. If you looked on one side, it was one style of building. If you looked on another side, it was a different style. And you bridged that together, so if you ever caught that magic corner of both, it still worked."

Because the back lot had to portray multiple sections of Iron City, Joyner says, "We worked hard to create a back lot where we could redress it and use it multiple times as different locations." Each building had an individual texture. "There are hundreds of selections of plaster application styles. We had a menu of textures to choose from that could be painted in a way that then gave them depth, dozens of different examples of technique and granularity and dust and knockout, where the building's been plastered over for the seventh time, and part of it's been chipped away."

As to why the practical sets are two stories high, Joyner explains, "That gave us the most coverage of the actors and action on the street, and anything that was wider or taller became a CG extension."

**THIS PAGE:** Photos of the Iron City streets sets (below) and with added reference elements, including Zalem.

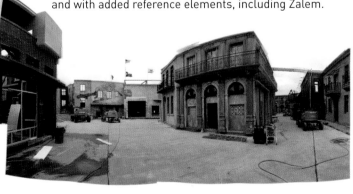

Much of the concept art depicts 3D set extensions that only exist in the digital sphere. "It's all done in conjunction," Cole explains. "Our back lot practical build was not yet built, but we had a design for it. It's not all just this colonial style. Sometimes there will be an art deco building thrown in there. This [3D artwork shows] that we would capture live action for the bottom portion, and then this [other area] would be a digital set extension."

Weta visual effects supervisor Eric Saindon explains that there is a 3D version of the practical sets in order to make the digital extensions work. "All of our stuff had to connect up with [the practical two-story sets], and be built back from there. We start from a space where there's nothing there, build our pavement, our sidewalks, and then all the buildings. We build it with a kit set. So we have twenty windows and we have twenty doors and all of these architectural pieces, and then we build various buildings, using different tools we have, to create the types of buildings that [Cameron] has in his artwork, and that Steve Joyner has built on set."

Reflecting on his *Alita* experience, Holland says, "I think this movie was more of a collaboration of design ideas than I've ever worked on before. Everybody brought things to the table. I miss it. It was a lot of fun."

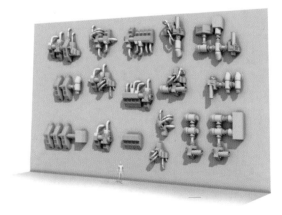

**ABOVE:** 3D concept design of sections of the supply tubes.
**RIGHT:** Concept art of Iron City at night, with the supply tubes running through it.

Iron City's buildings are connected by a warren of streets and alleys, where space is a major consideration. Holland remembers, "One night, Jon Landau started looking at what we had done, and he said that it just felt like our city was a little too open, a little too broad. Typically in cities, to have two lanes of traffic going both ways and a lane for parking, it's sixty feet [across], and then you have eight to twelve feet of sidewalk."

Holland reconceived the street width, with "a lot more nooks and crannies, cobbled together, much narrower. We had our streets down to twenty feet [across] at times. We wanted to keep it as tight as possible, so it looks very congested and contained. We had limited space, we only had a specific amount of time. We had to make it so that every view and every turn looked like a different part of the city."

"A lot of work went into designing the sidewalks," adds Joyner, "how wide they should be, how damaged they should be. On a lot of back lots, the sidewalks are just plywood that is painted over. Here, they were poured and then chipped away. We had one section where the plasterers went in and created their own cobblestones with cement and a trowel."

In order to accommodate camera equipment, there were a few "wild" removable building walls. However, "When you're building something outside, you have to build it pretty structurally sound," Holland points out. Each building might be dressed as several different establishments. "Each alley, even, could be shot from different angles to look different. So instead of an alley that has one entrance, we made a tri-alley with three entrances. If you look down it from different directions, it becomes a completely different alley."

Iron City trash had to be both convincingly grungy and futuristic. Holland relates, "There are tiles, there's glass, steel, bits of plastic, bits of old gears, discarded things that the next person probably would pick up and say, 'I can use this,' and drop something else."

**THIS SPREAD:** Concept art of the Iron City streets and street life.

**ABOVE:** Concept art of the Iron City streets and street life.

Cameron observes of Iron City, "It's got a lot of energy, but it's a very dangerous place. It's very slum-like in a lot of ways. It reminds you of a Third World city in Africa or India. And [its people] superimpose on that the relics of this very high technology that humans used to have, the cyborg technology. They're able to replace their limbs, even replace their whole body."

"*Alita* needed to fit into a technology of cyber bodies that developed in a couple of different eras, mainly a couple of hundred years in our future," Procter explains. "Obviously, the movie is set much farther in the future, but society collapsed [in the interim], and so you have the fact that people are cultivating old technology that's actually vintage for new purposes, taking care of old stuff, keeping it still running like new and combining old things together. So in Iron City, a lot of the tech that people are wearing is actually pretty darn old, [although] it post-dates us by a couple hundred years."

Not everyone has cyber enhancement, Procter observes. "There was discussion about how many people we'd see on the street who are [part or Total Replacement] cyborgs that went in a direction that was slightly surprising. It's meant to be no more than twenty percent of the people, just to keep it grounded. As far as the way those people look, we attempted to diversify what the change was to the body, make sure that there was a lot of diversity in age, too – there are kids with cybernetics, there are old people with cybernetics."

It was important to keep the cyber enhancements in line with the Iron City aesthetic. Concept artist John Park gives an example. "I was designing a prosthetic arm for one of the civilians that lived in the lower part of the city, and it felt too highly futuristic for the technology level, so I was asked to re-reference some of the 2005 artwork. But, more importantly, the selected reference materials, such as pistons, hydraulics and things like that, were a little bit more low technology. Originally, I was referencing things that were biomechanical, surfacing translucent gels, things that had complex surfacing, and it just didn't feel correct in this setting."

The cyber enhancements are treated by everyone as a normal part of life in Iron City. "There are people who dress like they just don't care whether the enhancements show or not," Procter says, "because we wanted to convey a hint of slightly downbeat realism. Jon [Landau] took a trip to Cambodia, and one of the impressions he came back with was that even though the people are really poor, they have a sense of fun and a sense of life there that is impressive. So that's kind of the notion, that [Iron City] people are just going about living their lives. They're in the ashes of a former world, but to them, it's the only life they have, so there's music and there's color, there's street art, there's always things happening. There's Motorball to be excited about. People don't just give up."

Costume designer Nina Proctor thought a lot about what sort of fabrics would be available 600 years in the future. "My theory is the things that are still going to be in existence are natural fibers, so I used a lot of cotton and linens and leathers," Proctor explains. "These people use recycled things, whether in set dressing, props or costumes. There are groups of people that we made specialty costumes for, but a lot of the background [extras] wear more found clothing,

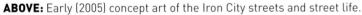

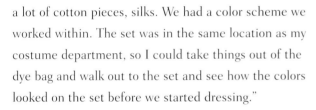

**ABOVE:** Early (2005) concept art of the Iron City streets and street life.

**ABOVE:** A guitar-playing cyborg street performer.

a lot of cotton pieces, silks. We had a color scheme we worked within. The set was in the same location as my costume department, so I could take things out of the dye bag and walk out to the set and see how the colors looked on the set before we started dressing."

For the colors, "I went with faded reds and purples and greens, oranges, browns," Proctor continues. "[Production designer] Steve Joyner's office is just down the hall from mine, and we meet at least five to ten minutes every morning, so he keeps me up to date as far as his color palettes for the production design, and I keep him up to date. We wanted to reflect the colors that are in the city. We also wanted to reflect all the different ethnic groups – people dressed in saris and longer pieces – but the main thing was reflecting that color."

Included among the background characters with cyborg limbs is a signature Rodriguez motif, a guitar player. While Rodriguez didn't actually suggest the character, he did respond strongly to the concept art depicting "a guitar player with cyborg arms playing a double-neck guitar," Rodriguez recalls. "I thought, 'We

can put together a guitar, and I can play the notes so that we have something to match.' That's the kind of stuff you have to pre-prepare, so that you have it ready on set. I actually played the reference music for that, because the actor we got didn't know how to play. So I did the arms and they're going to replace them with cyborg arms. That was fun."

Rodriguez didn't need to wear performance-capture gloves, he explains. "I just did it straight up, so that they could see where the fingers were going, because he doesn't have one-to-one fingers. His fingers are a little bit mechanical-looking. One hand is strumming, and the other hand is picking, and the other hand is doing fast arpeggios."

The Iron City taqueria set provides a special moment for Alita and Hugo, and had special appeal for the *Alita* crew as well, according to Eddleblute and Joyner. "When you're building something," Eddleblute says, "you want to know if it's really going to work. And as we would build certain sections of Iron City, we would see people congregate around them. Crew members would congregate at lunch around the

taqueria. We realized the city was actually coming to life. The taqueria was one of the grounding corners of the environment. We knew that the flow and the layout of it was working.

"The taqueria is reminiscent of [eateries in] all the places we've been, even the little colonial towns in Mexico," continues Eddleblute. "There was a specific photograph that I'd seen a long time ago, which showed an arched building with no roof, and it really appealed to me."

The production designers considered how long their taqueria could have been in business, and decided "It is definitely a repurposed area," Joyner says. "Over the years, it has been many things, so there are many layers."

The *Alita* production repurposed it as well. "It gets redressed several times," Eddleblute explains. "We pulled out the taqueria stuff and made it a little market corner, because you could see through it. [Visual effects supervisor] Richard Hollander had the team put blue screens behind it, so that he could create another section of the city. We tried to provide as many options as we could for each little area."

**ABOVE:** Concept art of Ido and Chiren in Iron City.

The little Iron City bridge where Alita and Hugo share a kiss is part of a consistent theme in the movie, explains Joyner. "They're trying to get elevated above the masses. Whenever they have alone time, we tried to give them a higher vantage point."

"In the script," Eddleblute elaborates, "we noticed that when Hugo and Alita are together, Hugo brings Alita above the fray of the city. In thinking about that early on in preproduction, there was a reference I really liked to a bridge that traverses a little alley of houses. We were able to incorporate that and build this little stairway that goes to the bridge above these shops. That's where Alita and Hugo have a nice moment together. It follows that thread of their moment in time together having an elevated quality to it."

**BELOW:** Concept art of Alita and Hugo on the "kissing bridge".

**ABOVE:** The "kissing bridge" portion of the Iron City streets sets.

# STREET MOTORBALL

When Alita ventures out into Iron City, she meets Hugo, who plays street Motorball with his friends on homemade ramps and skates in a courtyard. This encounter changes the fates of all involved.

Concept artist Messing says that when he worked on the street Motorball sequence, "I was trying to capture the kinetic energy of that raw version of the game, the tension of kids grinding, with sparks coming out. It's like any street ball game. [For reference,] we looked at tribal kids and we looked at slums, like New Delhi, where kids are running around in the streets and stuff, and even Cuba. It is a very raw, gritty, simple version of the game. The Iron City kids have their primitive version of the Motorball shoe, which we did a bunch of design versions of. But for the illustrations I did, it was more about the storytelling and the action in the street."

Concept artists must bear in mind where the emphasis should go in a scene. "It's very easy to over-render in detail

**THIS PAGE:** Concept art of Alita and Hugo at a street Motorball practice area.

something that doesn't matter," Messing notes. "That's a big problem of any big, wide environment shot, knowing how to simplify the statement of the image. We're always battling: 'That building would catch a reflection,' or we're going into all this detail on a background cyborg character, when those elements aren't the narrative focus in the shot. So it's always a question of knowing how to draw the eye to the right moment."

Even street Motorball isn't simply innocent fun. "The gladiatorial sport of Iron City is Motorball, and it's played at different levels, just like basketball is played from high school to college to pro," says Joyner. "Kids' Motorball is

emulating what they see on the big screens all over the city. There's huge enticement to become a [professional] player, so naturally the athletic kids are playing Motorball in the slum district of our city."

For the look of the skate ramps, "We have a steampunk infusion in the architecture already, so we didn't go too crazy," Messing observes. "We wanted it to look very practical, and like kids could put it together. So there wasn't any floating sci-fi stuff. Their roller skates were already kind of futuristic, so a lot of the construction of the ramps was very primitive. It was like bent metal, and then you have something that can go up the side of

**ABOVE:** Concept art of a street Motorball game at the courtyard skate park.

a wall, maybe at a more aggressive angle than a normal skateboarder could do right now, but we want to keep it somewhat grounded."

Hugo and his crew have set up their own ramps, which are based on real-world skate ramps. "In fact," art director Holland relates, "we contracted a bunch of professional skateboarders to build the ramps. They build them for different X-Games and things like that."

Eddleblute recalls, "We had a stage adjacent to us and set up all the skate ramps and worked out all their moves

for this large game sequence that the kids play while the set was still being completed."

"Stunt coordinator Garrett Warren had recruited all these skaters who could, without wires, do amazing flips and jumps and tricks off ramps," Joyner adds, "and from feedback of his test corps, he was able to tell us what kind of ramps he wanted, different half-pipes and jumping ramps, which we built. The ramps were conventional ramp construction, so it was ribs and plywood, with metal copings on the ground, so they could make the transition

to the ramps. It's pretty much the kind of construction you'd find in a present-day skate park.

For the skate park courtyard set, Eddleblute wanted a fountain. "They're great for light, they're gathering places," agrees Joyner.

Set decorator Dave Hack found a fountain design that pleased everyone. It was then made by *Alita*'s construction department, largely from concrete. Holland explains, "[The kids] needed to be able to jump on this thing and skate across it, to land on it. It needed to be sturdy. It has three levels, smallest at top, middle, and then a wide thing at the bottom. We studied different sizes. Sometimes we wanted that fountain out of there or to move it for the camera. So we had to make this thing 'wild'-able [portable]."

The fountain's look fits in with Iron City's colonial architecture. "It's not a modern fountain," Holland continues, "it's not any nationality's style, it's just a pretty typical fountain. It would fit in Europe, it would fit in Africa, it would fit in Great Britain. It would fit anywhere."

In Iron City, Joyner notes, the kids make their own street motorballs from found objects. "They're essentially leather-covered rubber balls. They don't have a motor in them like real motorballs. That's one of the differentiating factors between the amateur games and the pro games."

Then there are the skates. "Prop fabrication must

have built at least fifty or sixty pairs of skates of different designs," Joyner estimates, "until we got one that the producers and director liked, and that became the skate." The skates also had to look like they'd been assembled by their wearers from castoff materials. "That's part of the game. You have to find and build your own equipment."

For the skates' visual style, Joyner continues, "We looked at a lot of things. A few years ago, companies were really big into making off-road rollerblades, which are basically big-wheeled rollerblades that will handle a rough texture like grass or a dirt path. We looked at a lot of videos of those things, we looked at different manufacturers. In the current day, when you're rollerblading, you're powering the skates yourself. The kids' skates [within the story] are powered electrically internally, so we added motors and battery packs to the skate design. All of that was custom-made and fabricated."

The skates are all practical. "The kids are skating and they all have to work," explains Weta senior visual effects supervisor Joe Letteri. In order to make them look motorized, "We will overlay them with digital versions of the skates that look a little more futuristic than the practical ones."

Costume designer Proctor says her department had to buy skate shoes before any actors were cast. "You don't know if everyone's going to end up being a size nine or twelve. I probably ended up with maybe twenty pairs of them. They're skates that go right down the center, not four-wheel skates, but a little different than just in-line skates. And we got those early on. The skate model we chose had been discontinued by the manufacturer, so I ended up shopping on eBay to find these skates."

The skate motors operate in CG, but the stunts are real, Joyner reveals. "Garrett found a young guy who

**LEFT:** Photo of the street motorball.
**BELOW:** Concept art of Alita playing street Motorball.
**OPPOSITE:** Concept art of street Motorball skates.

**ABOVE:** Early (2005) concept art of Alita and Hugo at a street Motorball practice area.

could skate up a very small ramp – the ramp was only eighteen inches – and do a back-flip over this fountain that was about seven feet tall, land successfully and keep skating. I'm sure people will think they did it on wires or with VFX, but this kid was so good that he really was able to pull the stunt off."

"There were elements that we incorporated in the sets to help Rodriguez set up cool scenes," Eddleblute says. "We made sure that there was a steel banding around [the fountain], so the skaters could hop on and off of it."

Eddleblute recalls Rodriguez's reaction to seeing the fountain/skate park set, surrounded by Iron City buildings, for the first time. "The shadows were getting long. I remember him looking up and his eyes got big, and in that moment, he was like a total kid. I would see people walk through the back lot, and they were always looking with a sense of wonder. That told me a great deal about the environment working successfully as a narrative."

**RIGHT:** Concept art of street Motorball skates.

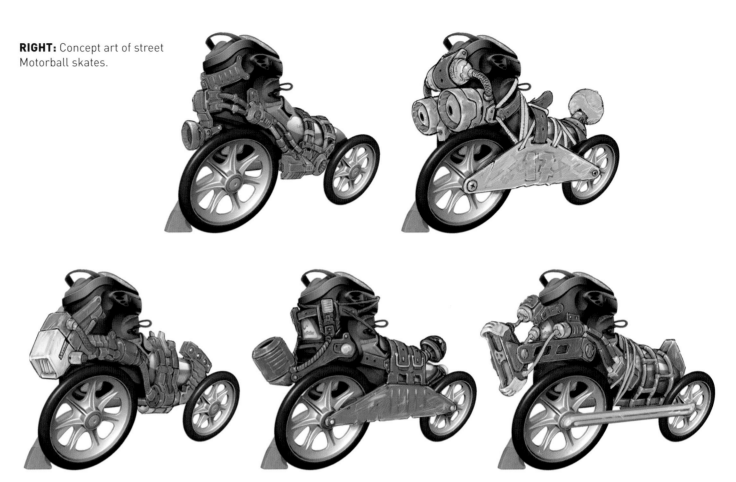

**BELOW:** Playing street Motorball at the courtyard skate park.

# BOUNTY KIOSKS

Bounty kiosks are run by the Factory and are where Hunter-Warriors go for the latest information on wanted criminals in Iron City.

"After looking at some beautiful concept art that [illustrator] Shane Baxley had drawn, we bounced a bunch of ideas back and forth," production designer Steve Joyner says of deciding on the kiosks' look. "There were tons of elements in his drawing that resonated with me and the tech 'language' we use for the film. I also borrowed some elements from Jim Cameron's design for the military equipment.

"We finalized the design and fabrication produced that kiosk in three days," Joyner continues. "The elements were cut on CNC machines here [at Troublemaker], and then it was painted by scenics. We picked out five or six [larcenous]-looking extras and said, 'Hey, we'll take your photo,' and those became the wanted posters that are displayed on the bounty kiosk. Those are throughout the city, so the three locations you see them in, it's the same bounty kiosk. Our original concept was, it was a futuristic open pay phone booth, that three-sided thing on a post, except this one dispenses bounties."

**RIGHT:** The bounty kiosk at the Kansas Bar.
**BELOW:** Two mug shots for the wanted posters.
**BELOW RIGHT:** The wanted poster for Grewishka.

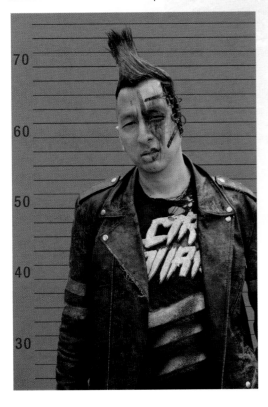

# SCRAPYARD

The Scrapyard is the area of Iron City into which the floating city of Zalem drops all its garbage. It is here that Dr. Ido finds the cyber core that he places into the body he had constructed for his lost daughter. "It's the debris of Zalem," production designer Steve Joyner explains. "They dump their garbage there, and people then can go in and root for materials, and a lot of that is recycled into products that go back up. So the Scrapyard is sort of the feeding of raw materials to Iron City."

"Steve [Joyner] and Richard [Hollander], the VFX supervisor, and I talked about what we needed for the Scrapyard," says art director A. Todd Holland. "I sat down at my computer and I worked up an idea that I had. I was just kit-bashing." Kit-bashing is a model-making technique where pieces from one model kit are glued into another different model to create a new look.

The practical Scrapyard set, Holland continues, "was based on two C containers on a stage, so it was about

eight feet wide by forty feet long, and this would give our hero movement to go in and out. We'd shoot it a couple different ways."

"We were very fortunate to have [set decorator] Dave Hack and [set decoration buyer] Jennifer Long as our set decoration team," Joyner says when asked where all the scrap metal for the set actually came from. "They turned us onto a place called Alamo Aircraft in San Antonio, which is one of the oldest privately-held scrapyards

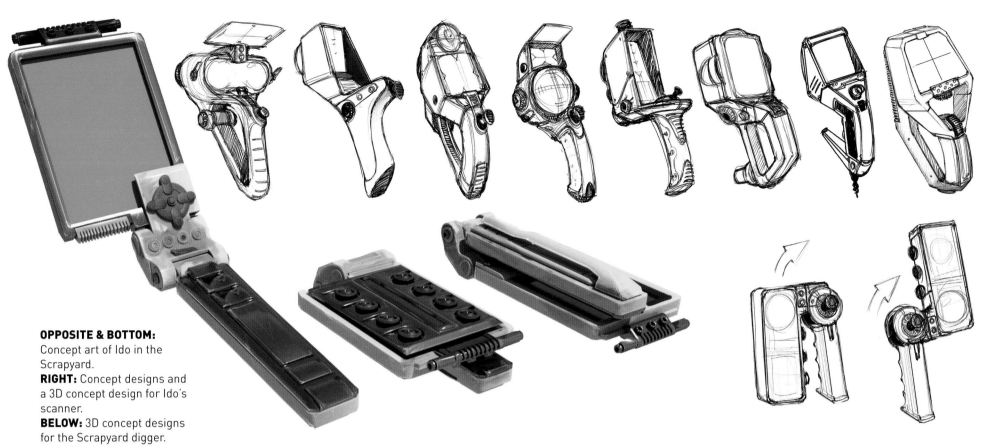

**OPPOSITE & BOTTOM:**
Concept art of Ido in the Scrapyard.

**RIGHT:** Concept designs and a 3D concept design for Ido's scanner.

**BELOW:** 3D concept designs for the Scrapyard digger.

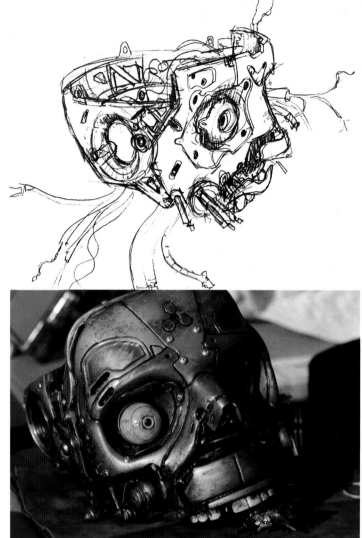

**ABOVE:** Photos of the Scrapyard filming set.

**ABOVE RIGHT:** Concept design and photo of a cyborg skull in the Scrapyard.

for military aircraft that you can still access. They have stuff going back to World War II there. They had beautiful, futuristic-looking but old stuff. We brought back truckloads of material from there. [There are] hints of shiny objects and things that pop out, but we were leaning towards the old, rusted iron for our Scrapyard."

The Scrapyard extends for miles, so "We extended the Scrapyard set drastically," in CG, Weta visual effects supervisor Eric Saindon says. "It went from a very small set to a very large setting." For that matter, "We pretty much extended almost every sequence in the movie," he laughs.

Production designer Caylah Eddleblute notes of the practical scrap pile, "We built an interactive set piece that Christoph [Waltz, as Ido] was able to climb and work through a section. Then we worked with Richard

Hollander to make sure that we and [cinematographer] Bill Pope could have a good digital extension and have these elements meld together properly and basically always have some sort of middle ground past the actors, so that there would be room for visual effects to make the extension."

In order for actors to safely move around within the practical Scrapyard while giving the illusion of clambering through an unstable mound, Holland explains, "I devised a simple set of ramps and steps that were a bit modular, and if we wanted to reconfigure them, we could. We configured it to have a couple different routes we could take, so it looked a little different if you flipped the camera around. If you pour a pile of sand down on a tabletop, it naturally goes to about a forty-five-degree angle. So when I designed the

steps, everything had a slanted forty-five [degree angle, with] a wood base. We would screw or pile little pieces of structure on top of that."

Sharp-eyed viewers may spot an homage in the Scrapyard to a previous creation of *Alita* producer/ writer James Cameron. Joyner reveals, "[Prop fabricator] Chris Wolters is a machinist and artist, which is a neat combination to have. For his college project, he made an exact replica of the Terminator arm from *The Terminator*. At his job interview here, he walked in and put that on the desk. It was such a beautiful piece, I said, 'You're hired. I don't need to see a resume.' For *Alita*, I asked him if we could borrow the arm and we tucked that among the scrap as an Easter egg."

**THIS PAGE:** Early (2005) concept art of Ido in the Scrapyard.

# THE CUTTING-EDGE TECHNOLOGY OF
# ALITA

*Alita: Battle Angel* is shot natively in 3D, rather than shot in 2D and converted to 3D in post. "Because Lightstorm was at the cutting edge of the 3D renaissance with the first *Avatar* film and part of blowing it up to what it is right now, we have a reputation that we have to maintain of doing the best 3D," explains James Cameron. "To me, the best 3D is native 3D. [Shooting 2D and] converting it later is automatically giving yourself a maximum of a B grade. The only way to give yourself the possibility of an A+ grade for 3D is to *shoot in 3D*. Not that many people do it, but the directors that do it – Martin Scorsese and Ridley Scott and Ang Lee – are amongst the best filmmakers. That should tell you everything you need to know about whether you should shoot native or not.

"Robert Rodriguez had shot native 3D before," Cameron continues, "so he was completely familiar with the rigs that Vince Pace and I developed. He already knew how to do it. That was almost a non-conversation: 'You doing native 3D?' 'Yeah, of course.' Which would have been a multi-week conversation with another filmmaker!"

To understand how 3D works, "Think of 3D as being a pair of eyes," animation supervisor Richie Baneham suggests, "but each eye is a camera. So you're rendering the subject [being shot] from two discrete perspectives, and the difference between those perspectives depends on how far apart the cameras are placed (the interocular distance between the two). Each camera is viewing the subject from a slightly different angle, with the subject of their perspectives being at the convergence point. It's the way the human eye works, and therefore how stereo [3D imagery] works."

Rodriguez has decades of experience with both CGI and the native 3D process. From camera operating to editing, he has done virtually everything involved in filmmaking at one time or another. "I'm used to doing all those jobs," Rodriguez acknowledges, "so it was great having Weta there on set [for *Alita*]. When I did *Sin City*, I was the Weta team. I had to come up with everything, because it was a very scrappy production, where you're the whole crew. So having these stellar resources was just unbelievable, and allowed us to move so fast. I'd say, 'Guys, you want me to get a clean plate of that, because I would be getting it to help myself later in post?' And the Weta guys would say, 'That would be great. But we don't want to bother you by making you do this.' 'No no, I know that gig.'

"We had to rig cameras everywhere for performance capture," Rodriguez adds about the CGI element of the shoot. "You have to pre-rig everything, to be there getting all the data, keeping track of each shot, because every shot is an effects shot. It was just so smooth. I thought for sure that whole system was going to slow us down, because it was such an army of people, but Weta have just got it down. We came in on schedule."

For *Alita*, Rodriguez explains, "We shot with the Alexa 4K dual-camera system – the best we have – for true 3D capture. You've got the A-camera on a crane and another team on the second camera, usually on a dolly or a smaller crane. Then the 3D guys are a different department. They're in their own tent, adjusting and doing the 3D as its shot. With the DP [director of photography] over in his tent, talking to all of them, telling them what to do. It was different from when it's just me running and gunning with a camera. It's a lot to organize. I'm watching and

responding and giving notes as it happens."

Although *Alita* marks the first time Rodriguez and Cameron have collaborated directly, Rodriguez has been using Cameron's 3D techniques for a long time. "I started shooting digital on the *Spy Kids* movies," he notes. "I was thinking, 'Digital is capable of so much, I wonder if I could just strap two of these cameras close together and shoot on greenscreen, and then in post, slide them closer together and create a sort of 3D?' I was doing a bunch of tests. Then Vince Pace [*Avatar* director of photography: LA, who also did additional photography for *Spy Kids 3*] said, 'Jim's already built this system.' I got Vince, who had designed these cameras with Jim, to rig up an over-and-under system, where we could shoot through glass and do the traditional 3D, but with digital, so we could see on set if it was working or not. That was pretty awesome and game-changing."

Rodriguez is also very happy to be working with director of photography Bill Pope. "I thought the work he did on *The Matrix* was stellar and visionary," the director enthuses. "I love to shoot with DPs. I learn a lot of good tips, seeing how they solve a problem. Bill was a joy to work with. The hard part when you're shooting a 3D movie and operating [the camera] yourself is that I'd have to run back to the 3D monitors, have them replay the take, watch it in 3D, then go back on set. It slows everything down. Bill was just so good that I don't think I ever operated the camera once, I was always watching the 3D."

There are often choices to be made as to whether something will be shot in practical 3D – using greenscreen or motion-capture reference – or be rendered entirely with CGI [computer generated imagery]. Rodriguez says this is usually "an individual call on each shot. There's stuff that we try to do practically, so at least we'd have reference. I like to have a reference of what an arm movement would look like, for example. We can always replace it if we have to, but we try to do stuff as real as possible."

Concept artist Steve Messing says of his part in the development process, "We do all sorts of things. We build 3D models, we have a drawing tablet that we can use to sketch, we use photography, we'll shoot photos of textures and warp them into perspective. For *Alita*, we even built primitive 3D models in the computer of the street set. We would take photos from a certain perspective of little Styrofoam core models of what we wanted to build for the set and paint over them to create an image. The visual effects team then made the decision whether to build models for it. Some stuff, they don't necessarily need full 3D models, it's just used as a frame of reference for the visual effects look."

The concept art informs the digital design, but it is not literally incorporated into the CGI. "We always build in the computer," Weta visual effects supervisor Eric Saindon notes. "Concept art is primarily [for reference], because it's only looking at the subject from one angle." However, when the subject turns within the computer in three dimensions, the new angles may present different aspects. "That's part of the process. We always have to build everything low-resolution first, as a quick CGI model, so that we can see it rotating, make sure everyone's still happy with it, usually make some changes, and then get back to making sure all the angles work for everybody."

Asked to give a layman-friendly explanation of how 3D builds are done within the computer, Weta senior visual effects supervisor Joe Letteri says, "Inside a computer, you start with dragging points and lines around, and you line them up into a 3D model. It's almost like building them out of a wire frame, where you start connecting points, as if you were drawing a triangle on a piece of paper. But then you rotate it around a little and draw another triangle that connects to it, and draw another one that connects to it. In this way, you start building up shapes. You start stitching all these pieces together and building it up in the shape of whatever you want. You have a lot of design tools to simplify that. You can take a circle and extrude it and make a cylinder, you can take a square and extrude it and make a cube. You are building and designing and sculpting inside the computer, so everything has three dimensions."

"The sketches and the artwork we get are a visual guide to what we can do, for example, telling us how big certain things are," Saindon says. "Then once we actually get it into our world, it needs a lot more figuring out in actual 3D space. We can't just pop random buildings into a city and visually make it work. Because it's a 3D movie, we have to build the entire city to get the visual representation of what [visual consultant] Dylan Cole has conceived in his

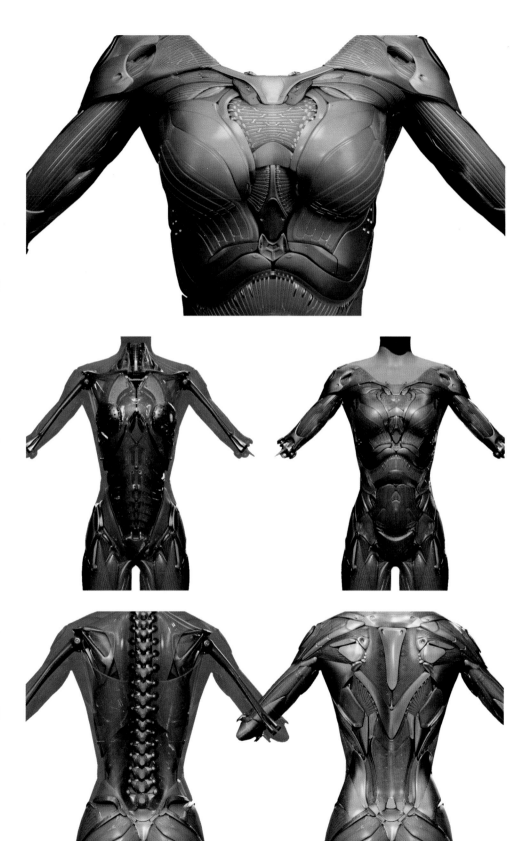

**ABOVE:** Weta Digital models of Alita's Berserker body torso structural detail and exterior.

concept art, and achieve the correct depth and the correct atmosphere, so we can see the city properly. We start with an empty space, then build our pavement, our sidewalks and all the buildings. We build it using different tools we have, to create the types of buildings that Dylan has in his artwork, and that Steve Joyner has built on set, matching the actual set construction."

"Because we're capturing the Alita character in all the different locations, we had to set up a performance-cap volume in all the locations," Saindon continues. "We would always go in the night before shooting, set up our cap cameras, so that we always had a volume to capture Rosa's motion. A volume is basically a space. We have a hundred or so cap cameras on set, all pointing at the same space, and that space is the volume."

There are different challenges in creating a human-style character like Alita as opposed to more cybernetic individuals like Grewishka or an environment in CGI. "Grewishka and the Motorballers all have to move in certain ways. The face – the eyes, the mouth, the nose – is obviously the first place you look. But the physical movement of those characters is how you-sell them," Saindon says. "If the design doesn't allow us to move the arms or the legs in a proper way and you can't sell the movement, the viewer will never buy those characters."

Regardless of how sophisticated the technology becomes, the creative human factor remains vital, Letteri notes. "A lot of it still has to get done by hand, especially for these characters. They're very individualized, and they're highly articulate. So you've got this unique design for an arm that's built out of old parts, but it has to function like a human arm does. It still has to be able to reach and twist and grab. So we have to think about how you're articulating this, as if you were going to build that as a true 3D robot arm in the real world. We just never take it to the point of manufacturing it. We finish it off in the computer. But it has to function as if it were real."

"The animation on the character of Alita is made up of a couple of things," Baneham elaborates. "Broadly,

we capture the body of Rosa for Alita. We do a [motion] capture process where the skeletal data in real-world space is extracted to digital [using performance capture suits and reference dots]. At that point, we start to make decisions about what it is that's specific about the performance that we want to hang onto, and what specifically we would augment or enhance. On the facial side of things, we do a facial capture, but then

we animate all of the layers on top of it. That gives us probably seventy percent of the performance in the basic capture. But the devil is in the details. The last ten or fifteen percent of the credibility of the performance is the most important. So that's the stuff you're striving for – how to make it come to life, how to make it feel real, and make it feel as if Alita has a soul."

To capture Rosa Salazar's facial performance, the

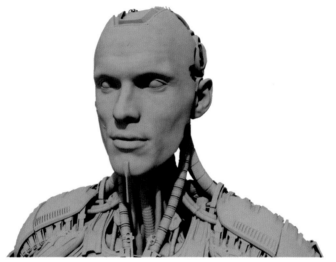

**ABOVE:** Weta Digital models of Zapan and Nyssiana's head and shoulders.
**BELOW:** Actual-size cutout of Grewishka used for reference on the Kansas Bar set.

**CLOCKWISE FROM ABOVE:** Behind the scenes photo of filming a scene; Prepping actress Eiza González in makeup for a Nyssiana scene; Filming a scene with McTeague (Jeff Fahey).

actress wears a "head-cam" helmet with a rig that has a camera mounted on it, pointed at her face, where makeup has placed a grid of dots on Salazar's skin. "The camera captures what happens at the skin-surface level, that matrix of movement," Baneham explains. "Then we willfully re-engineer the actor's facial movements [in the computer] to create a nuanced performance from Alita that feels real to the viewer."

There is a continual back and forth dialogue between the filmmakers, the VFX artists and Weta. "The process of going from concept art to finished visual effects is continually evolving," Jon Landau notes. "We don't turn [the art] over and say to Weta, 'This is exactly what we want.' They have to now build it. When we see Alita's face come to life, there are little differences in a static pose where you're not seeing her talk, you're not seeing the full range of expressions," Landau continues. "Those moments are when we really look at the detail of, 'What is the mouth doing?' Richie Baneham is helpful in all of this. We continually evolve it, not just as a design, but also sometimes on a scene by scene basis, so that we can get to that range of emotion in Alita that Rosa gave us in her performance. We're continually asking, 'What modifications do we need to make to get her performance coming across?'"

For non-human objects, such as the obviously mechanical cyborg body parts, "From a design standpoint, there is a utilitarian nature to the mechanics that need to be understood, and we worked with [visual consultants] Ben Procter and Dylan Cole on those to better understand what the intended look is," Baneham adds. "From there, we extrapolate what we think we can achieve based on the plates. We mark it in with Mike Cousins, the head of animation at Weta, and then we put it up for review and try to get a consensus from all of the key artistic players as to whether or not it achieves what they want."

Procter and Cole "have been heavily involved in the VFX reviews, looking at the assets. In my case, the assets of all the cyborgs as they've been developed, both as shapes and designs," Procter continues. "Not the animation – Richie Baneham oversees the performance animation. But as far as the mechanical aesthetics of how something moves, we all critique it together with Robert in his reviews. For example, [the animators] may come to us and say, 'We need [this cyborg character's] arm to extend really way up high, but look what happens to the piston in the scapular area when the character performs that action: it loses connection. What are we going to do?' Then we agree, 'We're going to add a pivot here, we're going to put a triple telescope on that piston instead of a double, based on the function they need.' Overall, the aesthetic is of trying to solve things.

"The way that the characters are ribbed reflects that, with pistons and motor housings," Procter concludes. "They tend to behave within the laws of how they should operate. If it looks real, and it feels real, we've given the right aesthetic intention to the audience."

The process on *Alita* involved an uncommonly high level of communication between departments, according to Procter, with the design artists, 3D artists, animators and filmmakers all conferring with one another. "Typical movie, you supply artwork – 'This is the intention' – and then people on the other end, usually without any communication with you, have to figure out how to make it work," he says. "In my experience, it's a little unusual that the *Alita* visual consultants are involved in the way that we are, looking at dailies."

**BELOW LEFT:** Filming a scene with Rosa Salazar's body double Mickey Facchinello as Alita.
**BELOW:** Final still from the same scene.

**ABOVE:** Concept art of Iron City showing how the physical set (not green) would be extended and Zalem added with VFX.

**BELOW:** Filmed still (left) and the final still (right).

# CYBORGS

"[Iron City is] a place where cyborgs and unaltered humans live side by side. There's no pejorative, there's no bad connotation to being a cyborg," says James Cameron. "In fact, if you have modified arms and legs, it's almost a sign of wealth. Then there's the highest end of cyborgs, the Total Replacements, where all you have left is your organic brain – your entire body has been replaced by a machine body that's bigger, stronger, faster, more beautiful, whatever you aspire to. In a sense, there is a level of status associated with being a cyborg."

Though having cyborg parts doesn't mean that the rest of a person's life is high-tech, Cameron adds. "It's all a very mature technology, and it's readily available in the same way that a farmer today will have both a cow and a cell phone. So there's a disparity between the technology that's available and people's living conditions."

Some people replace body parts that have been deformed since birth, others get cyber upgrades in order to make them better equipped for their jobs or for big-league Motorball. "It's just become a normal way of

life for people to have replacement hands, arms, legs," Cameron concludes.

In broad terms, the Iron City cyber aesthetic was derived from motorcycle parts. "I'd say if there was one photo-bash [blending several photos and/or painting over them] subject we scavenged the most, it was pieces of motorcycles," says visual consultant Ben Procter. "So certain people have the aesthetic of one kind of motorcycle, and other people have the aesthetic of another."

**THIS SPREAD:** Concept art of Iron City cyborgs and cyborg body parts.

Production designer Steve Joyner observes that "The [T-800] Terminator, designed by Jim, has a very distinct [visual] language. Our cyborgs are different. The question of how we were going to work to make that [aspect] different and unique came up specifically during our concept phase. So we eliminated hydraulic rams. We were using more linear motors and energy sources that were self-contained, so we don't have that look of, for example, a bulldozer. If you look at the T-800, he's like a piece of excavating equipment. If you look at the cyborgs in our movie, they're what's projected to be more the future, where the motors are all internal and part of the structure itself, without the rams and cables and pulleys. We

deliberately stayed away from a lot of glowing stuff. Jim and Robert's aesthetic is that there's a high-tech power source in the mechanism. Your engine doesn't glow in your electric car. It's all built in and part of the machine. That feels more grounded in reality."

"We made lots of different cyborg elements, some pistons, different arm bits," Weta visual effects supervisor Eric Saindon notes, "and we're using those to try to have many variations of cyborg arms and legs and torso bits and make sure we're seeing different cyborgs throughout the city."

Another variation can be seen in the delineation area between skin and technology, which indicates how

painless or painful the cyborg part is for an individual character. "With Alita, it ended up being a golden edge line around the skin," character designer Joe Pepe says. On less lovingly crafted cyborgs, "The skin is visible, but the layers could be visible into the core of the cybernetic layering. There is a framework that the skin lies on top of, over the cyborg. There are areas where you can see the cut line, you can see the thickness of the skin, whereas Alita has nice detailed edging."

Procter adds, "It's been an important discussion with Jim, that the way that these things attach to the body is not magical. So not taking the human ribcage and saying, 'You're going to support a fifty-pound

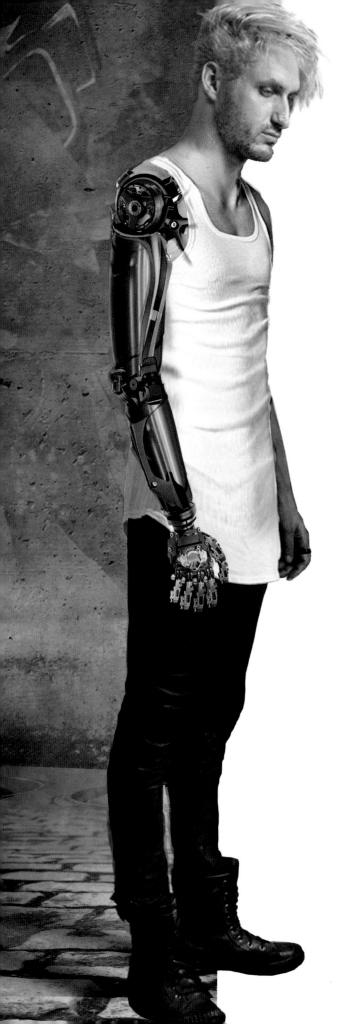

mechanical arm with screws into the ribs,' which would injure the person. Instead, the way that these things are attached is in a prosthetic way. So if you see somebody with a big giant arm, even if you can't quite tell, under their shirt, they've got something very much like an amputee's artificial arm cuff that goes around the stump of the body and has cross-bracing straps. On some of our characters you see those details, on others you may not, but still they're there."

The delineators, the places where cybernetics meet flesh, are a key element in the costume designs, costume designer Nina Proctor explains. "We had a mother walking down the street, wearing a tank top, holding her daughter's hand. The mother had a cyborg arm, so I did this delineator piece on her. It showed all the straps that would have helped hold that arm on.

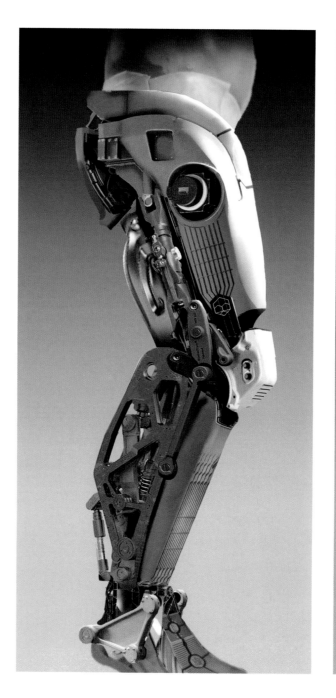

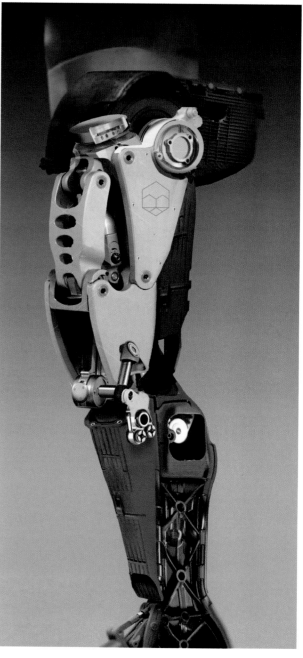

The arm is CG, but the piece was there to hold the arm in place, to help with the extra weight. So it was an over-the-shoulder strap piece, and you could see the strap going across her body, and over her shoulders. For the characters that have those pieces, I didn't necessarily want to cover those strap pieces up, because that becomes part of the costume.

"We had one construction worker character whose legs were cyborg," Proctor says. "I was able to do some pretty heavy-duty strappage on him to help support that extra weight, because the cyborg part is going to weigh more than [an organic] arm or leg. There's leather involved, and then the straps are heavy-duty nylon, at least two-inch-wide straps that came over his shoulders and connected to his legs. They crisscrossed in the back to help support that even more."

**THIS SPREAD:** Concept art of Iron City cyborgs and cyborg body parts.

# NYSSIANA

Nyssiana, played by Eiza González, is a jacker and one of Ido's Hunter-Warrior bounties, who uses a cloak to conceal her insect-like cyber body until she's ready to attack.

"Nyssiana is very similar to Zapan in the sense that the face is pulled directly from the actor," visual effects supervisor Richard E. Hollander observes, "then right around the jaw line, things change immediately and become mechanical. They're mechanical in different ways, but the overall process is the same – use their face, everything else goes."

Character designer Joe Pepe recalls, "I was given two images of [lead concept artist] Mark Goerner's 2005 concept art of Nyssiana that everybody already liked. That was more painterly, but with these praying mantis insect arms. So I built upon that with a photographic head and then I took a motorcycle faring – the fiberglass part on the outside of the motorcycle – and built the upper body, her torso and arms with those elements.

[Using an image of] a fashion model, I put makeup around her eyes and blackened her lips, so her lipstick is black or deep purple, and then I put some grooves into her face. I think the grooves have gone, because Robert wanted to have [her look] human upon first glance, but without her hooded robe on, she's cybernetic from pelvis up.

"I spent a lot of time with [visual consultant] Ben Procter, designing how her human legs connected to her cybernetic body," Pepe continues. "Ben had painted some ideas that I refined. Ben had done these great little separate shapes, the inner thigh to the outer thigh, different design elements, some with

stockings, some without stockings, but they all had a vinyl boot. In my illustration – I believe one of the final ones that we submitted – is a long vinyl boot with six-inch high heels, starting from her ankle going up to her thigh. A vinyl sleeve went over her leg. A couple of pieces that were like motorcycle farings came down over the upper thigh, and then transitioned immediately into a synthetic skin."

Even Nyssiana's skull is synthetic, Pepe adds. "Only her face is skin. It was an all-metallic skull, but the neck was made up of multiple pieces, so that there are a lot of negative shapes, so it looks like a head resting on top of this network of metal. Again, it's emphasising in the design that this character is a cyborg, she can't be a human actor inside of a suit. That's why her head is suspended, in a sense, over her body."

Weta visual effects supervisor Eric Saindon

explains that Nyssiana's sword-like upper limbs inform her fighting style. "She is more of a praying mantis, so that her arms fold up, but the blades are built into her."

To dress Nyssiana, "I designed a cloak, mini-length, with an oversized hood and longer sleeves, fitted in the upper arms but belling out at the bottom," costume designer Nina Proctor relates. "I chose a distressed lambskin red leather, with black details and hidden hooks and eyes down the center to keep it closed until we did the reveal. The leather reminded me of an aging paint surface where you can see the old layer of paint coming through the cracks. She wears black hose with tall black fitted boots. The hose are paired with a custom-made leather garter with heavy metal connectors. This serves as a delineator where her legs connect to her upper body. Once she starts her fight with Ido, she loses the cloak [and Gonzalez] is dressed in the grey performance-capture suit."

**THIS SPREAD (EXCEPT LEFT):** Concept art of Nyssiana.
**LEFT:** Eiza González in Nyssiana makeup and full mocap suit.

# ROMO

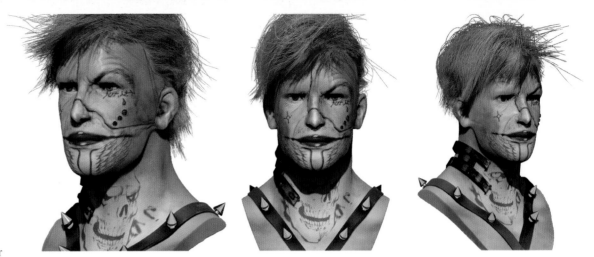

**CLOCKWISE FROM ABOVE:** Concept art of Romo; Photo of a Romo prosthetic sculpt.

Romo, played by Derek Mears, is a jacker, someone who steals cyber body parts off the living in order to sell them at a profit. While his partner Nyssiana is a Total Replacement cyborg, or "TR," meaning that she is completely mechanical except for a human brain and brain stem, visual consultant Ben Procter says, "Romo is a little more ambiguous. It's possible that he's more of a partial. He also has some skin grafts. There are some areas where you're not quite sure if that's cyber skin or human skin, or both. We generally try to be orthodox with the cyborgs in *Alita*, as far as most of them not having both types of skin directly next to each other, but Romo is one of the few characters [who blur the lines]."

   In terms of CG elements, "Romo and Nyssiana are pretty much the same," Weta visual effects supervisor Eric Saindon relates, "using the actor's real head, and putting it on a CG body. We captured the two of them in the performance-capture suits through the Ambush Alley sequence. Though where Nyssiana has blades built into her body, Romo has blades he holds."

   "Romo's upper body was cyborg, designed with all these tattoos," costume designer Nina Proctor says. "I dressed him in custom leather pants with heavy zippers on either side, instead of one zipper at center front. I also created a rather large leather studded codpiece and heavy-duty studded belt. This was grounded with heavy-duty leather boots. I wanted his clothing to reflect the style of his upper body."

   Production designer Steve Joyner reveals that Romo's weapons are some of his favorites in the film. "He has a collection of knives that [prop fabricator] Chris Wolters sculpted and shaped by hand from steel and aluminum that turned out fantastic. His weapons weren't found objects, they were made by design, based on the character concept art and the original manga. We tried to honor the original author as often as possible with the weapons designs. For the fight sequences, the fabrication shop molded those [blades] and was able to make safe rubber copies. For the actor Derek Mears, who's the sweetest guy, his weapons really helped him get into that villain character."

**FAR RIGHT:** Photo of Romo's knives.

# KANSAS BAR

The Kansas Bar, where the Hunter-Warriors hang out, is the location for a big brawl in the movie. "The bar fight was such a big element in that first [manga] book, and in Jim's script," director Robert Rodriguez recalls. "It was a ten-page bar fight, and it was fantastic. I couldn't wait to do it. I said, 'I've got to nail this, because this is such a big section of the movie. So I've got to do my homework. What bar fights are there? I want to make sure we're not repeating something that's been done.'"

When reminded that he and James Cameron are responsible for a few of the best ones, Rodriguez notes with a laugh. "I wouldn't have even thought of that, but I did a search for 'best bar fights in movies' and found a Top Ten list that [included] *Terminator, Terminator 2,*

*From Dusk Till Dawn* and *Desperado*. Jim said, 'We're four of the Top Ten bar fights, so we've got to do a good job on this. This has got to be the best one of all our movies put together. This is our thing.' [Jim] actually visited on the day we were shooting one of the bar fights, and that's the best time to have him visit.

"You realize as you read the scene, it's not about the fight, it's about the characters," Rodriguez continues. "Alita is walking into a deadly situation to trigger a memory, and she's going to start a fight with the wrong people and it's going to turn out badly. It starts off as her showing off and a celebration of her antics while she beats everybody up and throws them around the room. Then her [adopted] father Ido shows up, then Grewishka

shows up, and it gets really dark. So it's already got built in drama and conflict that puts it above the normal bar fight, which is usually just, somebody comes in, says a dirty word to someone else and they start fighting. This has a lot more going on, because of Jim's groundwork. So it's not about the actual fight, it's about everything leading up to it and everything that comes after. As long as we've got some really cool moves of Alita's to show her off – and that's what's great about her, she can do anything, and she can bounce around and dodge and slither in and out of situations – that's fun. You haven't seen a little girl doing all this stuff. But the drama that goes around it is really what's going to separate it."

Asked how action for cyborgs is different than

**THIS PAGE:** Street level exterior of the Kansas Bar.

**ABOVE:** Early (2005) concept art of the Kansas Bar interior.

desperado, vampire, hitman or spy action, Rodriguez replies, "Cyborgs can do things that others can't. They have superhuman strength and they can break things, so those characters are fun to choreograph for. You can throw people around quite a bit."

Appropriately, the practical set used for the Kansas Bar, Rodriguez reveals, "was a redressed set of the TV series *From Dusk Till Dawn* bar set, where I'd staged a bunch of other bar fights."

For the bar's design, "This is another case of looking at page counts and actions," production designer Steve Joyner says. "We knew we wanted the Kansas Bar to sing. One of the concepts that struck me at first was, there's a bar in Austin called the Elephant Room. At street level,

you have a set of stairs that lead down, and it's kind of unique in that. Also, that follows the manga. The Kansas Bar is an underground bar – literally underground."

Production designer Caylah Eddleblute adds that it helped to be able to work from a standing set. "Between art director Leslie McDonald and her wonderful tenacity, and [illustrator] Shane Baxley, who came up with some great concept art, we were able to create a set that worked with the environment that we had existing already. We changed the position of the bar, we fabricated beams that went from the floor through the ceiling. I imagined it as being like the underground of an old monastery where they had the wine cellars, and the tradition carried through to it being a drinking

establishment at this junction."

"The Kansas Bar is very rough and tumble," art director A. Todd Holland says. "We kept most of the walls, kept most of the size of the space [of the *From Dusk Till Dawn* bar]. We redid the floor, we redid some parts of the walls, we added the brand new bar, we added the stairs, we put in big architectural new elements that would be holding up the bigger buildings way above us, big steel girders. The walls were primarily stone. The floor was actually all wood."

Joyner recalls, "One of our art directors found a place that was scrapping tractor-trailer rigs, and there were scraps of aluminum with these giant one-inch-thick oak planks that made up the floor. We bought them all and turned that [planking] into the floor of the bar. It's got this beautiful beat-up old wood with lots of holes in it."

"Since a lot of fighting was happening, throwing down on wood is much better than on a concrete floor," Holland observes, "and Grewishka cuts up the floor with his razor claws and they dive into the floor. So we needed to make it a floor you could break through, and wood seemed like the way to go." Granted, the break in the floor couldn't go very deep in reality. "Since we were using a set that initially had been on a concrete floor, you could only break through the floor just a few inches," Holland adds.

For furniture, the Kansas Bar "had it all," Holland says, "barstools and tables and benches and cubbyholes. From our hard aircraft salvage, we would take parts of

jet engines, flip them upside down, weld a couple more things on it, put a tabletop on it."

Joyner elaborates, "[Set decorator] Dave Hack, [assistant set decorator] Bart Brown and [set decoration buyer] Jennifer Long found a bunch of great piston airplane engine frames and turned those into a lot of the furniture and set dressing pieces in the Kansas Bar. The [metal] tables were pretty tough, but Bob Trevino, our mechanical effects coordinator, built tons of balsa wood chairs. Those broke a lot [in the fights]. In the middle of this high-tech bar, we had some balsa chairs for [stunt coordinator] Garrett [Warren] and the stunt players to play with. It made the bar fight spectacular."

There's no pool table, but the patrons of the Kansas Bar do play cards. "We made two different, unique

sets of decks of cards that our property master Jason Hammond took care of," Holland reveals. "Our graphic designer, Ellen Lampl, did some symbols and new styles of fonts, with different numbering and shapes."

Eddleblute observes that the Kansas Bar exterior, part of the larger Iron City set, is "beautifully-built, lined with arches and a little breezeway. This was another building that played as several different settings that would be redressed. Everything would play as a market one day, then be the Kansas Bar at night."

The Kansas Bar also has a distinctive sign. "Fabrication cut that with a CNC plasma cutter out of steel," Joyner recalls. "We had two, one on the outside and a really big one on the inside…"

"Lit from the back," Eddleblute concludes.

**THIS SPREAD:** Concept art of the Kansas Bar interior.

**CLOCKWISE FROM ABOVE:** Concept art of Grewishka and Chiren entering the bar; A view down the covered walkway outside the bar; Electronic wanted posters sit on the bar's tables.

# KANSAS BAR PATRONS

The Hunter-Warrior customers in the Kansas Bar are as tough as they come, and the majority have cyborg body parts.

"Because most of them are ex-Motorballers [all of who are cyborgs], we got designs for all of the main characters in the Kansas Bar," Weta visual effects supervisor Eric Saindon says. "For the patrons in the background, we put individual [cyber] arms on each one. Each day, as we brought these guys onto set, if they had a mo-cap sleeve, we always made sure we got photos of them." This way, the visual effects department can determine later which character should get what sort of cyber appendages. It doesn't affect the action. "We let them do whatever they're going to do, and we'll put our CG arm over the top," Saindon adds.

Costume designer Nina Proctor calls the Kansas Bar patrons "a variety of badasses. We had a lot of stunt players, and each one is their own character. I would do fittings with them and try to personalize each character. We used a lot of heavy-duty accessories. Some of them have long full-length coats on, some of them have shorter biker-style jackets. I always tried to really age the leather or take it to another level, like you would see in a biker bar."

Some of the costumes needed to accommodate "flying wires," which are used to move stunt people whose characters are being thrown around. The stunt department make their own harnesses for the wires, then, Proctor explains, "we cut and slice that wardrobe wherever we need to, to fit those pick points [where the wires connect to the harness]. Each rig is a little bit different, and it fits on each person a little bit different. So usually, after they get dressed, they just tell us where those pick points are exactly and we're able to put holes in the clothing exactly where they need to be. "

There are a variety of women in the Kansas Bar. Some are Hunter-Warriors, some are girlfriends of the Hunter-Warriors, some are waitresses and some are prostitutes. "We have quite a few female background people in the Kansas Bar," Proctor notes. "I mixed it up. If it was a dress, I didn't want it to look like just a contemporary dress. I would change something about it through the use of accessories, or maybe a dress that you would normally wear high heels with, I would put them in biker-type boots.

"The girlfriends look sexy, but they don't look quite like the working girls. Sometimes their outfit reflects how the boyfriend is dressed or where they are in the bar. I'm actually able to go in and say, 'This person would be better over here, and this person should stand over here.' The assistant directors are great about letting me place people where they need to be.

"The waitresses aren't exactly alike, but their costumes were all made from the same fabric. It's gun metal in color and it looks like [it has] metal studs, but it was just sewn into the fabric. I probably made four or five different styles. They all have a similar, really short skirt. The tops look like somehow they all got hold of this fabric and each created the top that they wanted. Some are halter-style tops and some are off the shoulder. I did different types of leggings and tights on them, and socks under the knees. They all have the same style boot, a wedge heel in black with a silver metallic thread through them, just to ground the costume."

**ABOVE:** Patrons (Nick Epper and Jamie Landau in the foreground) and staff in the Kansas Bar.

# ZAPAN

Zapan, played by Ed Skrein, is an unusually vain Hunter-Warrior who has spent his fortune on his face. He becomes a formidable foe to both Alita and Hugo.

Lightstorm character designer Joe Pepe worked on Zapan with pre-visualization artist Chris Olivia, who was at Troublemaker Studios. "He and I went back and forth," Pepe relates. "He would do some things that Robert would like, I'd modify it some more, I'd go back to them, they'd modify it again. A lot of that started with 2005 artwork of this mechanical Mayan-feeling body. It looks like English armor, but it has a Mayan design on it. I think it stayed that way throughout the whole thing. The majority of my work with that was on the head and connecting the existing body. We used a reference face [in the artwork], until they cast Ed Skrein. Then I took all the same elements and put Ed's face in it."

Zapan's hair went through a lot of changes, Pepe adds. "I think Robert had initially sent me an image from the manga with loud, spiky hair. Once they got Ed into the performance-capture suit, they sent me some frames, and they wanted me to try a long Mohawk. Then I tried the greasier look of the Mohawk, a wavier one, and then a spiky one, and then a

**THIS PAGE:** Concept art of Zapan.

different height – short, medium and long. They gave me four different frames from two different scenes, so I'd do short hair, medium and a long hair of each of these different styles on each of the different frames. We gave them something to work with that we were going to see in the final film, instead of just a random illustration we had done. It's still the shorter-to-medium Mohawk, and it's a little bit thick and greasy."

Though he's a Total Replacement cyborg, Zapan is rich enough to afford human-looking synthetic skin. "Onscreen, you're supposed to be able to see the wealthier and the poorer distinction when it comes to synthetic skin," Pepe explains. "Some of it looks more waxy or shiny, and then more expensive looks more human."

With the rest of Zapan's body, visual consultant Ben Procter says, "He takes the decorative, showoff aspect of cyber-body design to a very fine level. He's got these Mayan calendar motifs all over him, embossed and etched in him. It's almost like the evil counterpoint to [Alita's] doll body, heavily decorated with a lot of style. There's a vanity to [some] cyborgs in our world – it's not just the guy on the street who has the Factory arm that lets him support his kids."

Costume designer Nina Proctor didn't make much wardrobe for Zapan, but, "I did have to create a cape piece for him," she says. "I thought, 'Okay, his body is steel,' so I found this piece of fabric that was almost like chain mail. It had a bit of sparkle and great movement to it."

"His chest is not clothed at all," Weta visual effects supervisor Eric Saindon notes, "and his lower half is a combination of [CG] wardrobe/design on his pants. It's leather that is integrated into his body, so it blurs the line between where his wardrobe stops and starts. We've made a 3D version of Aztec symbols on his metal plates, and that's what replaces his performance-capture suit. We've taken Aztec patterns and pushed those into metal plates in CG, and that's what makes up his back. We've pushed those same Aztec patterns into the rest of him, too, so that his metal surfaces have a bit of that Aztec

**ABOVE & BELOW RIGHT:** Concept art of Zapan from a scene no longer in the film.
**BELOW:** Final VFX shot of Zapan (Ed Skrein).

design pushed into them."

To make Skrein's head look persuasively attached to Zapan's digital body, as "In almost all the cases of the Motorballers," Saindon elaborates, "we've taken the filmed elements of the actor on set, we roto[scope] – which means frame by frame painting out everything except for their head – and then put that head back on a CG body."

Producer Jon Landau and director Robert Rodriguez both cite Zapan when discussing the importance of negative space in making the cyborgs look more realistic. "You can see through his neck," says Landau. "That's not something that you could have [with a live-action character]. We use Ed Skrein's face, but we digitally put in his neck and we see behind what would be there."

The negative space also allows for new moves in action sequences. "Alita grabs Zapan by the trachea," Rodriguez explains, "a place you couldn't grab a human. He probably never thought somebody would do that to him, but she can stick her hand in there and then she pulls him down in a way that really takes advantage of the negative space on his body."

Saindon adds that, when it comes to negative space, "For us, the most difficult part is putting back what wasn't there. We want to really sell Zapan as a cyborg by giving him negative space – you see the background behind his neck, so there would be no doubt that it's a CG character.

"We had to paint back whatever was supposed to be behind Ed [Skrein], because Ed is a big guy. He filled that part of the screen," Saindon continues. "So we always had to make sure we had clean background plates without Ed, so we could paint back what was supposed to be there. We never had [footage of] the action behind him, though. So sometimes when he's walking through a crowd, we have to make it up. Adding enhancements behind him, it's a tricky thing. We've had to add heads and things like that, floating back behind him in places where we didn't have anything to put back there."

Most of the time, Saindon says, these additions are digital, rather than from live footage. For one thing, the proportions with live footage cannot be controlled as easily as they can with CG. For another, "You just don't know what it should be. Live footage, the only way we could do that is to really go out in the parking lot and film ourselves, and put that back there. We've had to do that in the past, but not in this movie."

**BELOW:** Concept art of Zapan.

**BELOW:** Early (2005) concept art of Zapan.

# MASTER CLIVE LEE

Master Clive Lee, played by Rick Yune, is one of the Hunter-Warriors who hangs out at the Kansas Bar.

Costume designer Nina Procter really enjoyed working on his costume. "I custom-made it," she says. "It is a version of samurai warrior armor, with tweaks. Sometimes samurai pants were almost like full skirts. I did more like a jodhpur, which is an English-style pant. It pooches out at the thigh and then comes back in. Then we custom-made several pieces on the top out of all of these really rich textures of brown. He has armbands that we made in the shop that are hand-tooled leather, six or seven inches wide, like a gauntlet without the glove part. He has a vest piece belted around the waist. I made him a dark chocolate-brown linen shirt that piece was supposed to go over, but when we were doing the fitting, the vest piece fit the actor so beautifully, like it was sculpted to his body, that we decided to just axe the shirt. It really showed off his arms."

As a partial cyborg character, Master Clive Lee's costumes were designed so that they wouldn't be a distraction from the cyborg textures, Proctor observes. "The art department had made these really heavy-duty shoulder pads that he wore. They were a little flatter than some textured things that you find, so it gave me texture, but didn't get too crazy with it."

**LEFT:** Master Clive Lee (Rick Yune).
**ABOVE:** Concept art of Master Clive Lee.

# McTEAGUE

McTeague, played by Jeff Fahey, is a Hunter-Warrior who frequents the Kansas Bar with his pack of cyber-hounds. He was concept artist John Park's first character assignment on *Alita*. "It was such a blast, designing him, and really getting into what I would like to see as his visual background, and how the character relates to his dogs," recalls Park.

For McTeague's cyber look, "A lot of verbal direction was provided by [visual consultants] Ben Procter and Dylan Cole," Park continues. "Specifically, we were asked to look at sections of dye-cut machines, the underside of vehicles, things that were mechanically heavy in terms of reference, and take it into a design fusion, putting it into the character and making it believable from a functional standpoint. Also, to dress the character with things that would fit that Old West archetype: cowboy boots, and a hat.

"Thirty to forty percent of McTeague's body is mechanical prosthetics. The character has an entire [cyber] bottom jaw. I wanted to place the body parts in a way that was functional, not just purely mechanical for the looks. If you look at a car chassis, I'm using some of its elements as a reference. For example, a suspension could be represented as maybe a scapula or some sort of muscle to provide movement or strength. We looked at lots of those as cues to replicate the human body. So when you look at the visual design, you know that's not a human arm, that is a mechanical arm that's inspired by a vehicle or machinery that's been reconfigured."

**ABOVE:** Jeff Fahey as McTeague with two of his canine friends.
**BELOW:** Concept art of McTeague's cyber-hounds.

In designing McTeague's jaw, Park explains, "You would start with the general shape and the proportion of a human body part and then you would figure out exactly the mechanics of, 'Does this thing actually open? Is there a hinge?' And then we would take it a step further and see how we could apply this mechanical detail on the human flesh. So it was a three-to-four-step act. We wanted to find a balance."

"One of the things we tried to do was integrate the costume with the cybernetics, which isn't something I've seen done a whole lot," Procter says of McTeague's costume. "The McTeague character looks like a cowboy. We tried to take cowboy boots and a cowboy vest and integrate mechanical elements into them, so that it's all part of the fabric of what he looks like, as opposed to it just being a robot body wearing clothes."

"We are replacing his lower legs, we're replacing his chest and his arms," says Weta visual effects supervisor Eric Saindon, explaining how McTeague is realized in CG. "We leave the actor's head, but we're replacing his chin. Then we're replacing his arms with pistol-like shapes, so you actually see bullets from like an old six-shooter."

Although actor Fahey has often worked with Robert Rodriguez before, Saindon points out that performance-capture scans are not like prosthetic makeup, where unless the performer has changed drastically, old molds of an actor's face can be used for designing new pieces. "In CG, we start from scratch each time. It's always a new scan and a new version of that CG character."

Park designed McTeague's cyber dogs alongside the Hunter-Warrior. "They're meant to be reconstructed dogs. They're not a hundred percent robotic," Park explains. "There are biological elements of them that were left intact, but, for example, I had a dog's paws or legs completely replaced with mechanical details. We wanted dogs that had strength and a powerful stance, German Shepherds, pit bulls, Dobermanns. I looked at dogs [that have] prosthetics and human prosthetics. I also looked at theme park animatronic characters, before they [have skin overlaid on their forms], where there are

**ABOVE:** Concept art of McTeague with his cyber-hounds.

a lot of mechanics. That was a huge point of reference for me to understand how much complexity I could actually get away with."

A real dog was used for performance capture, playing all the members of McTeague's pack. "The cyber dogs are all designed based on artwork we got," Saindon says, "but it's going through the same process that we went through on the Motorballers. We built this design in 3D and then put it through motion tests, and then had to change the design to get it to move properly. We had a dog we put a mocap suit on, and we'll do performance-capture with a dog here [at Weta] in New Zealand, and we'll use that to drive our CG dog. We've put the dog in the suit a few times, so he's used to it, though it's more about putting markers on the dog than putting him in a suit. We also tried a dog backpack on him that has some extra markers on it, so that we can capture the motion."

# GREWISHKA

Jackie Earle Haley plays the massive, disturbed cyborg Grewishka. Director Robert Rodriguez says he wants to put Haley's audition video as a special feature on *Alita*'s eventual Blu-ray release. "He's a terrific filmmaker/director in his own right, so he shot an audition of himself with one of his kids operating [the camera]. They had the camera low, and he walked around and was just so terrifying and menacing and had such rage."

In a non-CG film, Haley would not be cast as someone huge, but "As Jim [Cameron] said, 'This is a full CG character. Size doesn't matter. We want somebody who's got great acting chops.' And Jackie is someone I've always wanted to work with,"

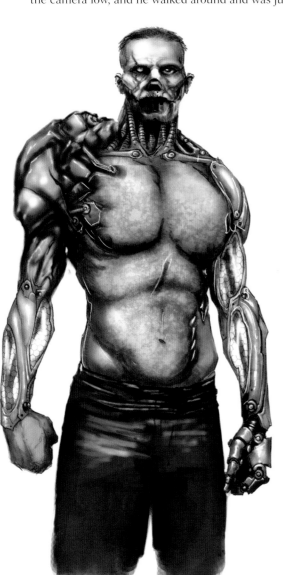

**THIS PAGE & OPPOSITE BOTTOM LEFT:** Concept art of Grewishka in his first body and his cyber core.

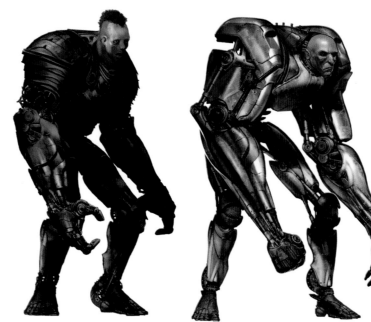

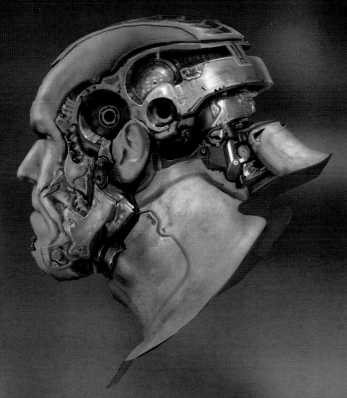

Rodriguez states. "We've always talked about doing something together. He sent this audition tape in, and it was spectacular. Jim said, 'We don't need to look any further.' I agreed."

Regarding Grewishka's look, "The concept art was really good," Rodriguez continues. "Jim had adapted the character already quite a bit in his [2005] version. All these *Avatar* artists [at Lightstorm] are so fantastic that the art they would send would be jaw-dropping and the speed at which they can do concept paintings is staggering. 'Okay, this looks fantastic. Maybe not a tattoo there…' It was an embarrassment of riches."

Weta senior visual effects supervisor Joe Letteri recalls, "When we scanned Jackie, we tried to take his

shape and blend it into Grewishka. That allowed us to bring Jackie's personality through, because he's got a distinct way of playing the character. He comes at it a little bit from the side, especially with his dialogue. We wanted to get that into Grewishka.

"But Grewishka has the added complexity of his head being embedded into the cyber mechanism," Letteri adds. "Whereas Alita has her [human-like] head and neck, Grewishka has a very mechanical neck and piece supporting his jaw. So we had to figure out what Jackie's performance is, and then modify the design of all these mechanics, like the pistons in the neck, so that they could follow his performance in a believable way. You don't want to

**ABOVE:** Concept art of Grewishka's head.
**BELOW:** Photos of a Grewishka cyber core sculpt.

**THIS SPREAD:** Concept art of Grewishka with his second, Grind Cutter Claw body.

lose the body posture and the tilt of the head and the eyes when he's doing his dialogue. So we had to back-engineer the design to support that."

Character designer Joe Pepe credits visual consultant Ben Procter and concept artist Fausto De Martini with doing the bulk of Grewishka development art. "I came in at the end, and took Ben's original illustration of Grewishka's head and face, and did a series [of images] with Jackie Earle Haley. When you start applying the features of the actor, everything has to change – the size of the jaw, the size of the cheek, the skull, the ears – so it was another series of back and forths with Ben, and then with Robert, who would illustrate on top of things, showing us what he liked. Everybody liked Ben's illustrations, so it was just making sure that the right percentages of Jackie's facial features came through."

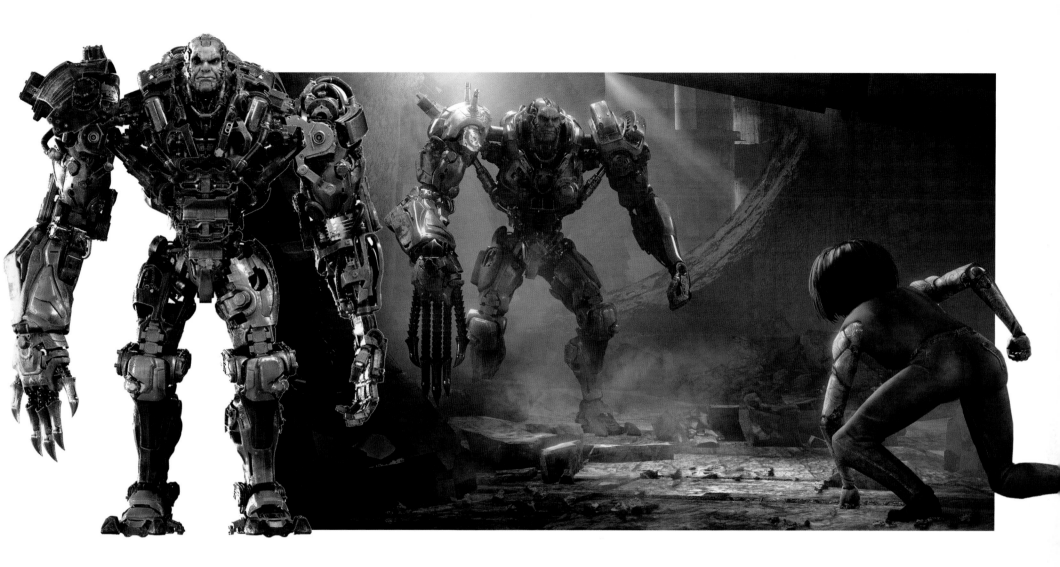

Visual effects supervisor Richard E. Hollander explains the techniques used to turn Haley's face into Grewishka's visage are the same as those used to transform Rosa Salazar's face into that of Alita. "They're two different [character] faces completely, but the actors are driving a set of geometry. The same facial-capture techniques, the same body-capture techniques are used. Then Weta has their internal tools that they apply. There's more Rosa in Alita than Jackie in Grewishka, but you *can* see Jackie's face in Grewishka."

"We've had to retarget Jackie's motion to a much bigger body and slow it down, so it feels a lot bigger," Weta visual effects supervisor Eric Saindon adds. "He obviously has a different gait than someone who is nine feet tall. We can take Jackie's motion on set and

stretch it out, so instead of taking five frames to do a step from one place to another, if we make that fifteen frames, then he looks like he's got a lot more weight and he's ripping up his foot and then putting it down. The original Grewishka obviously had no Jackie in it, so he's gotten redesigned since the original phase to add some elements of Jackie into the character."

In terms of Grewishka's myriad components, Letteri reveals, "For the body textures, there's a lot of metal, meant to evoke recycled parts and parts that have been part of something else at one time and then reassembled into these new forms. Most of it is steel, aluminum, titanium, painted metal. There are plastic pieces, a lot of tubing and cables, braided wire, the kind of grille work that you might find in motorcycle parts. Most of what's

in [Grewishka's neck] are pistons, but there are also a lot of tubes. Those tubes are meant to look like either nylon wrap tubing or braided metal tubing. The pistons themselves have some bare metal work showing. For the most part, it's steel, but there is a little bit of bronze in there to give it accent, or some aluminum. It all tends to have a patina, or been painted and the paint has worn down, or there will be grease stains on it. It's always a mix of source material and whatever we could do to age it, in all of his forms."

"Grewishka is unique in certain ways, because he's a hit man," De Martini observes. "When he was put together by Vector, he needed to be this machine of destruction, so there were some liberties that we could take to make him more aggressive-looking. It had a

  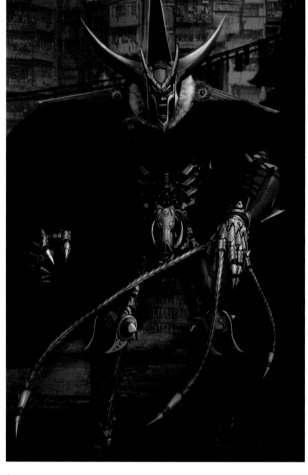

**ABOVE:** Concept art of Grewishka in his first body.

**ABOVE:** Early (2005) concept art of Grewishka in his second body.

lot to do with the thickness of the neck. Jim wanted something different than what was done in 2005. We sat down to look at the manga designs, [but] the parameters come a lot from Jim. Jim wants to make sense of the mechanical parts. Jim is one of my favorite [people] to work for because of that. He is not only artistic, but also an engineer, so he knows so many aspects of building things in general that it makes his feedback really precise and effective."

In the course of the film, Grewishka is virtually destroyed twice, only to be rebuilt. "There are actually three versions," De Martini says. "The first version was done by Ben. He established the face and body, which is almost rusty-looking. After he gets destroyed, there's a second version, which looks a little more silver. That's

the version that I developed. He looks a little more like specific parts were built for him, less hacked together."

Saindon explains, "Grewishka Mark One is part cyborg and part human. In Mark Two, he is replaced a lot more with mechanical bits, and gets a bigger body, so he's a foot taller." For Mark Three, "He's really wide, has much bigger muscles, much bigger arms, legs, everything."

"The face is pretty consistent throughout the versions," De Martini observes. "But for the [second] version, since the body had to be redesigned, I started from scratch, respecting the overall proportions that Jim brought up, like being triangular and having long arms. Ben said, 'I think we need to add some asymmetry to the body,' so you have a tube that goes here, but it's not on this side, to create that. He also has [one] more

human arm, but his right arm is longer and he has the Grind Cutter Claw that Hugo jacked from Kinuba that can extend, so this creates a lot of asymmetry. The legs are machinery, [but] are pretty human, proportion-wise. Even though they're not big, they had to be thick enough. The design has to look like he can actually move with a proper distribution of power and weight. I used a lot of anodized metal, and there are some specific scorch marks in Grewishka's chest area, because we want to give an impression that some of the stuff was welded. We kept the range of the metals pretty broad, but we always sourced from real mechanical parts. I think a cool mechanical design has to have a lot of metal variations, so there's a lot of copper and iron. Most of his armor was this almost silverish steel."

**THIS IMAGE:** Concept art of Grewishka in his second body.

**THIS PAGE:** Concept art of Grewishka fighting Alita in the Underworld.

In all of Grewishka's forms, De Martini continues, "The chest and torso area would always be closed up [to protect] the mechanical core, but I suggested to Ben that we put three hydraulic pistons to give him an interesting-looking shoulder. It's just the regular car piston, but there needs to be a good rotation system at the base. It would be very mechanical-looking, but also give a nice negative space."

Costume designer Nina Proctor made a cape for Haley's stunt double as Grewishka. "He is seven feet tall," Proctor remembers, "and then they put him on stilts, so he was nine feet tall, wearing KNB-molded shoulders, neck and head piece. The shoulders were about a foot wide from front to back. The cape was nine feet from shoulder to floor, meaning it was about eighteen feet finished, 240 inches wide in the upper body area and approximately 500 inches wide at the hemline. It was made from vintage army tent fabric and then waxed. The tent fabric was old and tattered and very frayed. I took advantage of the frayed pieces and incorporated that into the look of the cape. The cape was also hooded. I used super heavy-duty zippers, and then added a series of chains to the left shoulder area. Robert wanted to see that huge shadow coming down the alleyway. The cape was super-effective for that."

De Martini worked on the artwork of the moment Alita triumphantly cuts Grewishka in half. "Because

**THIS PAGE:**
Concept art of Grewishka in his second body.

**ABOVE & BELOW:** Concept art of Grewishka's final confrontation with Alita.

I work a lot in 3D, I ended up cutting the whole design in half, but then, as soon as [Grewishka's interior] was exposed, I was like, 'Okay, I'm going to have to show the brain, I need to show the core,'" De Martini explains. "The core contains the head and the spine and the heart and some other components. So I needed to make sure to show this core pretty clearly, showing the segments of the spine and having the half of the heart there, and other engine parts. I also had to design all the nice glowy bits, because when someone is cut in half with an energy sword, you're melting where the sword goes through. [There were] guidelines from Jim and Robert about the fact that the head and brains are the only things that are organic. Everything else was replaced by mechanical bits. So it was cool to do an illustration of that, because I was able to help design a little bit of the heart."

# UNDERWORLD

"It's below the Kansas Bar, where Grewishka and Alita have their first big fight," says visual consultant Dylan Cole of the concept art he did for the Underworld, the remnants of centuries past beneath Iron City. "They fall through the [Kansas Bar] floor and land in the bowels of the old city. It's drippy and moist down there, the old massive steel industrial infrastructure of the city.

"I will use photo elements, but it's not like I start with a single photo. I blocked each image in 3D," Cole continues, explaining how he created the art. "I used Cinema 4D, and I blocked in a lot of the pipes and shapes, and put some rough lights on it, but then other elements are great Photoshop [with] some digital paint techniques. I created the whole environment as a big 3D layout."

Art director A. Todd Holland elaborates on the design of the Underworld area where the face-off takes place. "We wanted to have a way for characters to get down there. Obviously, Alita and Grewishka can jump down, but Ido has to climb down. That architectural element that we had coming through the floor, basically holding up the buildings above, had to go down to the foundations. So we extended that same steel girder through it, and that was our architectural tie-in to this underground sewer. They could climb down it using the rivets, and then the steel, to the old sewers under the floor."

The Underworld includes "some pipes, but it's concrete and there's a big sewer area that's clogged with old discarded items and little bits where water streamed through," Holland continues. "But we're rock bottom down on the floor. It's whatever bit of concrete foundations are left from whatever subway or underground sewer was there 200 years ago."

Clearly, nobody wants actual sewage on the set. The materials used instead are "burlap, different bits of metal and rubber that we found, skimmed from the same architectural things and then painted to look like it had been through the wrong stuff," Holland explains. "Gross to look at, but it's just paint. We have fantastic scenics, led by [paint supervisor] Mike Mikita, and he came up with rust coloring, and sludge, and bits of dirt. We used a lot of ground-up rubber tires used in children's playgrounds. It comes in charcoal grey. It's safe, it's soft, it's clean, it looks wonderful on camera, and it cleans up very nicely. You can even fight on it."

For the practical set, "This was a partial set that was extended in CG. We built the floor of the Underworld that they fight on, and one wall of it was a big drain opening that Grewishka escapes into," production designer Steve Joyner says. "Construction built large beams that Ido and Hugo climb down on from the hole that we created in the floor of the Kansas Bar."

Because it's very dark in the Underworld, cinematographer Bill Pope had to be especially careful to light the sequence realistically. "Where was the light coming from? That was a question early on," Joyner recalls, "and Bill, working with John Sandau, our gaffer, constructed special soft boxes to give that very soft, non-directional light that allows you to see the action but lets dark areas fall off."

As to how deep the Underworld goes, Holland reveals, "It's meant to look unknown."

**MAIN IMAGE:** Concept art of Grewishka and Alita in the Underworld.
**RIGHT:** Early (2005) concept art of Grewishka and Alita in the Underworld.

# VECTOR

Vector, played by Academy Award®-winner Mahershala Ali, is the most powerful person in Iron City. He lives atop the Factory, is a key player behind the scenes in professional Motorball and even has a secret connection with the fabled city of Zalem.

"He hadn't blown up yet when we cast him," James Cameron says of Ali. "I had seen him in *House of Cards*. You can't take your eyes off him whenever he's in a scene; you want to see how he's going to play the moment."

Character designer Joe Pepe wanted to give Vector a unique look and put him in "a Hindu wedding jacket. I had never seen one before and I was attracted to its intricacy. I changed the color, threw it on his body, and put a different pair of slacks on him. It was dark maroon and charcoal."

Costume designer Nina Proctor describes her version of the garment. "It was made from a silk that came from Syria. Unfortunately, the market that it came from was destroyed. I'd had this piece of fabric for probably ten years, saving it for just the right moment, and it ended up being the perfect thing to make this robe. And then

I customized the pants that went with it that were a little bit fitted around the ankle, to give it a different look from a man's trousers today, and then a little bit of fullness that came through to the legs."

Proctor notes, "Vector is maybe the only person in Iron City who has money, or really shows his success." To reflect this in his wardrobe, "He has a very sharp look, very clean lines. At one point, he wears a below-the-knee custom-made coat without lapels. It is made out of black wool, but a wool that you would make a man's suit out of, not like a cashmere wool coat. It has a beautiful grey stripe that starts at his shoulder and goes diagonally across his body, and then it mirrors it on the other side. It has a really cool angle."

Ali was nominated for his Best Supporting Actor Oscar® for *Moonlight* while working on *Alita* art director A. Todd Holland recalls. "The assistant directors had a lot of fun with him. When we called, 'Please bring Mahershala to set,' they would say, 'Please bring Academy Award®-nominated Mahershala Ali to set.' He took it very well, in stride, because he is a very nice guy."

**LEFT:** Costume design for Vector.
**BELOW:** Concept art of the paralyzer lances used by Vector and his bodyguards.

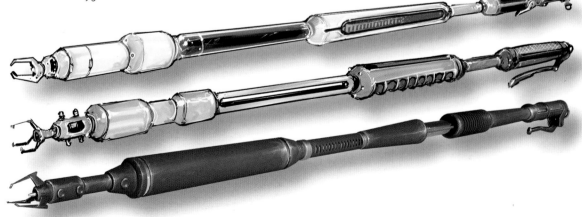

**ABOVE:** Concept art of Vector talking to Hugo in the Motorball stadium pits.
**LEFT:** Concept art of Vector's bodyguards.
**RIGHT:** Vector (Mahershala Ali).

# VECTOR'S LIMO

As befits its mysterious, menacing owner, Vector's limo is a unique and imposing vehicle. A lot of thought went into the ride's design. "Vector's limo went through a ton of iterations," concept artist Jonathan Bach says. "We were trying to go for something early on that was based on gyroscopic machines. We have a gyroscopic motorcycle [elsewhere in the film], and we wanted to do something like that for Vector's limo as well. So instead of doing a four-wheeled car, we went with a two-wheeled car that would balance on its own with a gyroscope, just like the motorcycles are gyro cycles."

Bach experimented with the shape and placement of the wheels. "I did try a few different configurations, but the one that was always more favored was a single spherical wheel in the front and the rear, a wheel with a hubless carriage. The wheel is pretty wide. We had the idea that the limo could move sideways and diagonally at will. So it could be a big vehicle, but in the tight streets of our city, it wouldn't have as much problem maneuvering as it looks like it might. If you wanted to park, you could just move laterally sideways. The intention with it being able to move laterally as well as forward and rear without having to turn was so Vector can make an entrance, where the limo could come sideways towards somebody, the doors would open and he'd just be presented in a very special way, rather than him stepping out of the car."

The practical limo, "has working doors that open like a minivan, front and rear on one side," Bach continues. "It's self-driven, so it has a stagecoach feel. Some of the iterations that were done felt coffin-like. It was armored. It was meant to be a street vehicle, but also very utilitarian and military and robust. It's configured like a lounge, so it's a C-shaped seating arrangement. The

exterior is asymmetrical. The window wraps outside to the roof, and then there's a pillar that runs behind that. It's sort of like a panoramic window, so everybody who's got a seat has a decent view out the window."

The tires exist only in CG, but the rest of it was built in Austin. Production designer Steve Joyner recalls, "That went through the concept design phase. Everyone, the producers, the director, agreed that they liked it, and at that point, we went to visual effects and said, 'Well, what do you guys think? Do you want to do this as a visual effect?' [Visual effects supervisor] Richard Hollander said, 'No, because people get in and out of it. Let's build it practically and we'll do the wheels as a visual effect.' So it came to us for Jeff [Poss]'s crew to build it at his company, PBE Exhibits. The key player in that was [illustrator] Shane Baxley, who reworked the two-dimensional lines to create very beautiful three-dimensional curves. We printed small 3D models of them, which then went to the producers and director to approve, and from there, we were able to take the 3D models that Shane did and Jeff's company actually produced full-sized fiberglass parts for them. They built working doors that opened and closed on it, they built a beautiful interior for Mahershala. That vehicle moves on skateboard wheels, which will be erased by Weta and replaced with the beautiful wheels that you see in the concept art."

"The skateboard wheels are set up so it's got four sets of four," Joyner explains of how the skateboard wheels worked practically, "and then four wheels go on a track. That allows it to ride on the track, so it works like a train car, and the vehicle looks like it's gliding."

**TOP RIGHT:** Concept art of the interior of Vector's limo.
**RIGHT:** Photo of the practical interior under construction.

**THIS PAGE:** Concept art of Vector's limo.

# VECTOR'S PENTHOUSE

Vector's penthouse sits atop the Factory, reflecting his literal and figurative position above the masses of Iron City.

"We stuck his penthouse in this Brutalist-style Factory," visual consultant Dylan Cole says, "and then we shoehorned in a bit of art deco. These buttresses [along the penthouse] reference the Brutal buttressing we have on the exterior of the Factory."

"Vector's penthouse was initially conceived as two separate sets and [production designers] Steve Joyner and Caylah Eddleblute had done some wonderful mood boards," recalls art director A. Todd Holland. However, for reasons of both space and budget, the set needed to be condensed into one. "I sketched it out," Holland explains. "If you look down in a planned view, it is in a 'V' shape for Vector. Then I built it in the most skeletal fashion

in SketchBook. The time from concept to approval by Robert was hours, which is very unusual. We developed it much further from there over the next few months."

The design allowed Holland to "be in the bedroom and look across the patio into the office, and it looked like a bigger space. Rather than four walls, I could put a bunch of glass, and then a space, and then more glass. So it had a grand view. It was a practical solution as well as an aesthetic solution. It had grandeur and it had a long, narrow quality that would fit on any of our stages."

In terms of décor, "Vector is cold, harsh, a violent man," Holland says, "so everything was glass and metal, angled and sharp. We incorporated his 'V' in monetary wealth ideas. For example, the sconces are diamond-shaped. All the handles on the glass doors are two sharp

angles, but placed in the walls to form a V, so when he steps back and the doors are closed, there's a subtle 'V' right there. Obviously, he thinks very highly of himself. Vector is putting his stamp on everything."

Vector's bed had to look expensive but cold. "That was a challenge," Joyner says. "We used dull metallics and hard lines and simply the massiveness of the bed implies Chiren's loneliness when she's left alone in it."

Eddleblute adds, "We had a prototype size for the bed that we brought in to the bedroom. We were all there, Steve, me, A. Todd, and [set decorator] Dave Hack. We had a mattress and built a frame around it, but we realized the bed was scaled just a little *too* large. We brought it down a little bit, and it seated in the room perfectly with all the other elements."

Cinematography was also a consideration in the design. "The other component that really sold that environment was [director of photography] Bill Pope's lighting," Joyner notes. "It was a very cold lighting scheme, and it came to life once Bill lit it. We had to pay attention to the reflections, so we used a burnished stainless steel that gave that very cold light without mirror-like reflections occurring."

"You need your surface to be just matte enough to please visual effects," Eddleblute observes, "and have just a hint of reflectivity to please the DP. We designed and built our own light fixtures for the penthouse and had discussions with visual effects supervisor Richard Hollander and Bill Pope to thread that needle. "

To address these aspects, Joyner says, "We designed Vector's windows tilted downward, so he could look down upon the city. Visual effects need to be able to pick up the reflection on the interior of Vector's face in the glass, but [also] show this CG effect of the skyline of the city in the matte painting outside. Instead of picking a blue- or greenscreen, Richard called for a black screen, so [rigging key grip] Pete Stockton could completely enclose the exterior of Vector's in stage black. That gave us the interior reflections that still allowed VFX to put the matte painting in on the outside." It also prevented unwanted reflections. "We thought we were clever facing the windows down, but we realized that it also gives you a really good reflection of the ceiling, so we had to fill that in," Joyner adds.

Within Vector's office, Joyner continues, "He's got a deco wet bar that construction and fabrication built, [which] transforms into a refrigerated body parts storage interior. It was modular. We removed the internal bar section and put in a refrigerated section that ends up containing the harvested parts of a character that are sent up to Zalem. [Special makeup effects studio] KNB provided us with hands, eyes, and 'salvaged' organs for that."

**LEFT, RIGHT & TOP RIGHT:** Concept art of the interior of Vector's penthouse.

**LEFT:** Concept art of the wet bar transformed into refrigerated body part storage.

# FACTORY

The Factory is the biggest hub of industry in Iron City. Under Vector's management, the Factory facilitates the unceasing flow of goods from the planet's surface to Zalem above.

The vast Factory complex is designed in the Brutalist architectural style. Visual consultant Dylan Cole created some early images "just selling the concept of the Factory, the industrial foundation of the whole city, where everything serves the Factory. We tried to create all these pipes and tubes as the circulatory system of the city, if you will. It all connects to the Factory; it's all functioning to serve Zalem."

There's a lot of cement in the Factory exterior to emphasise "the corporate Brutal element in that," explains production designer Steve Joyner. "Actually, that was [art director] A. Todd Holland's homage to the bottom of the Geisel Library in San Diego. It has a very Brutal line to it. He turned that ninety degrees and used it as an exterior finish. The set inside is based on a piece of concept art from Mark Goerner, who was one of the lead concept artists for Jim in 2005."

Much of the Factory is CG. For the practical build elements, "We did the doors, floor and big interactive part of it and the table at the end," Holland explains. "The doors are massive. We went for really big scale, with a subtle Factory motif on the front. We wanted to show Alita, who's not a big girl to begin with, pushing on these doors. We did a good section of the floor, but [VFX] will extend it visually so it looks a lot longer. We just wanted to show scale from that, and a bit of sleekness, that this is a more untouched, cleaner environment once you walk through the doors. There's some color – they added some bronzes, things like that – there's some warmth, especially in the floor. It wasn't as cold and sterile as a surgical room.

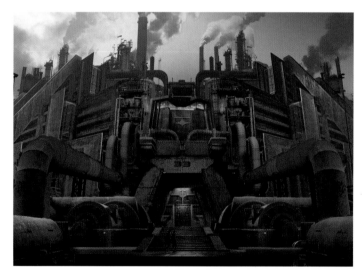

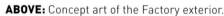
**ABOVE:** Concept art of the Factory exterior.

Outside, it's dirty, it's dusty, it's a difficult life, but the Factory shows a more elitist, cleaner environment. People still go in and out of these doors, don't get me wrong, but [the Factory interior] and Vector's apartment are the cleanest environments."

For the Factory floor, "Marble was too expensive," Joyner says, "so it's a beautiful [paint supervisor] Mike Mikita faux-finished stone that has a great deal of reflectivity in it, but not too much."

Production designer Caylah Eddleblute recalls that cinematographer Bill Pope "got down to eye level with the floor, to make sure the surface was not too hot and not too matte. It was just right."

"That took some careful finishing by the scenics," Joyner adds. "We had to protect the floor the whole time, right up 'til shooting. From there, [visual effects supervisor] Richard Hollander and the Weta team take it over and extend the set."

**ABOVE:** Concept art of a Factory freight truck.
**BELOW:** Concept art of the Factory interior, including Centurions.

# DECKMAN

When a Hunter-Warrior bags a criminal, they deliver the severed head to a robotic Factory Deckman to collect the bounty.

The Deckman went through a number of design concepts. In the end, Weta visual effects supervisor Eric Saindon says, "He's pretty much a little pod that pops up from a unit. He has some dialogue, but it's very simple motion. He doesn't have lips, so it's just a flapping mouth."

In terms of how the Deckman receives the bounty's head, "That's a spinning-top shape," art director A. Todd Holland explains. "It floats off the ground and extends out. It has a couple of arms that stick out. The Hunter-Warrior talks to the Deckman, puts the head on the scanner and it scans it, tells them how many credits they're going to get, and then the trapdoor retracts so the head can drop in. That was actually one of our cool special effects practical moments. The [Deckman] head that talks to them, that will be VFX, but everything else was practical."

**ABOVE:** Concept art of Ido collecting a bounty from a Deckman.
**BELOW:** Photos of the Deckman filming set.

**ABOVE & RIGHT:** Concept art of the Deckman.

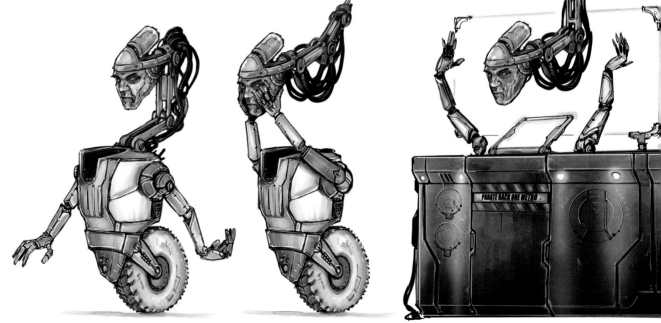

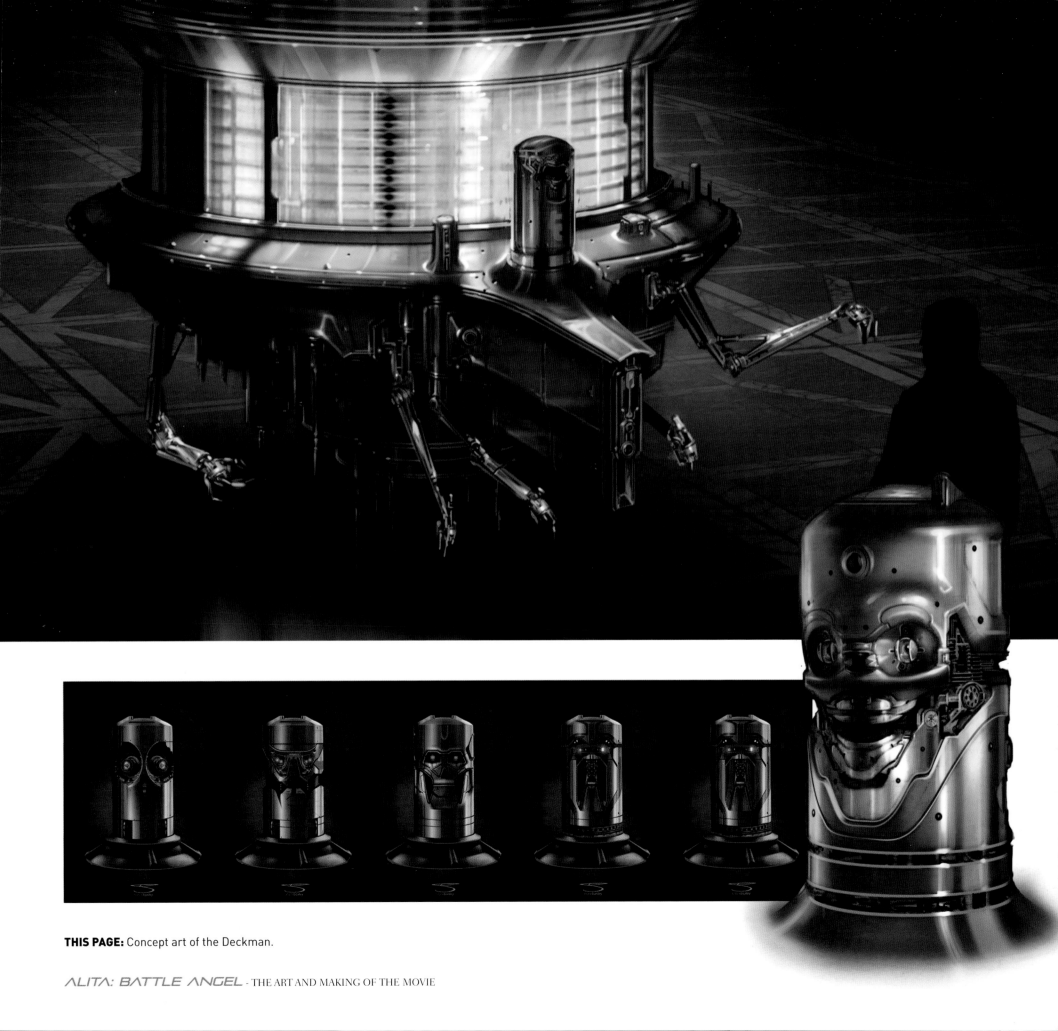

**THIS PAGE:** Concept art of the Deckman.

# CENTURIONS

"The Centurions are all CG," explains Weta visual effects supervisor Eric Saindon of the multi-legged machines that make sure no one acts against the Factory's best interests. "They're the police for the city. They're Factory Artificial Intelligence. They walk around the city, controlling the city."

"A lot of people worked on the Centurions," says production designer Steve Joyner. "I think that pretty much came from the description in the script. [3D artist] Alex Toader spent a lot of time developing the look of the Centurions, and he did a great job. They're the enforcers of the Factory's will over the people.

"Stompiness was a factor, for sure," Joyner adds when asked about the considerations in designing the Centurions. "They are basically walking tanks. We followed the rule of, they need to be narrow and tall to move through the streets, and they don't police the city so much as just enforce the will of the Factory to make sure that the goods are flowing freely to Zalem. They have no human personality at all, and they were designed to be intimidating."

**ABOVE:** Concept art of Alita saving the stray dog from under a Centurion.

**THIS SPREAD:** Concept art of the Centurions.

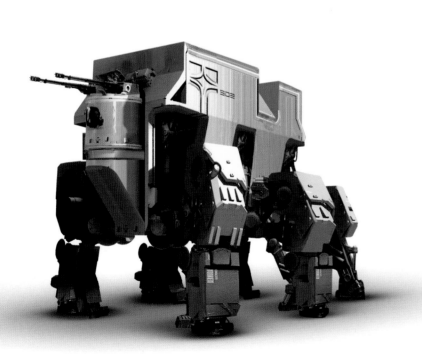

# CHIREN

Chiren, played by Academy Award®-winner Jennifer Connelly, was exiled from Zalem and is a skilled cybersurgeon, like her ex, Dyson Ido. Chiren now finds cold comfort in the employ, and bed, of brutal Factory boss Vector, who she hopes can help her return to Zalem.

Character designer Joe Pepe explains that visual consultant Ben Procter did the initial research on Chiren's look. Pepe then began his work on Chiren based on this, well before Connelly was cast.

Chiren's hair went through a number of conceptual changes. "We went through a bunch of blonde and brown hairstyles with Jennifer," Pepe says, "and also with the jewel in her forehead. Basically, they're like hair and makeup tests, but on a photograph." Experimenting with different looks digitally means that the actor and the hair and makeup department don't have to do practical tests. In the end, it was decided to go with Connelly's natural dark hair coloring.

There is a striking jewel in Chiren's forehead. In the concept art, Pepe says, "I ended up picking a cut amethyst. That was based on the manga." It is the only part of the final character that gets a little CGI help, to make it twinkle.

Costume designer Nina Proctor describes Chiren's look as "classic. She was a hard character to figure out – not just as a costume designer, but I think it is a little bit difficult for Chiren to find who she is in her world. She does not want to be in Iron City. She works for the bad guy of our story, creating TR cyborgs and pushing the envelope. She doesn't know completely what this relationship with Vector is. She had been married to Ido – she is divorced, but in some way, she is still drawn to him. What I ultimately did was to feed off of Vector and his world, because Chiren is so much a part of that world."

**BELOW & OPPOSITE TOP:** Concept art of Chiren.

**LEFT & RIGHT:** Costume designs for Chiren.

To emphasize Chiren's alienation from her surroundings, as well as her elevated financial status that comes with augmenting professional Motorballers, Proctor had a strategy. "I always wanted her to stand out, like she is so misplaced in this world. The first time we see her, it's a busy street scene. Everyone's in their rags, and here she is in this dark, navy blue dress with a 1940s feel to it, but very contemporary, too, very fitted at the top. She wears a blue fur with that, over the shoulder, not a long piece that hangs down, it actually fits her around her shoulders. Then she has three-quarter-length sleeves, and the navy blue gloves that go with it. Everything is really put together, down to navy blue shoes."

Chiren has a different but equally striking look when she's at work in her lab. "I wanted her lab to look so different from Ido's lab," Proctor says. "Ido is like the neighborhood doctor and anyone can come in. Chiren is all about making the Motorball players stronger and stronger. We wanted that feeling of everything being sterile. Her lab is very clinical, so I wanted to reflect that in her [costume]. Her lab coat is tailored, a very pale blue. Underneath her lab coat is all white, even down to these stark white shoes that have a futuristic feel to them. They have this odd-shaped chunky heel on them. I usually avoid white, but with all this new technology, we can use white a little more freely than we used to be able to. Film used to really blow white out [visually]. Shooting digitally, you have more control over that. The lighting works really well with the white. We have her in the lab in two or three different looks, so it isn't like she wears the same uniform every day, but she always uses that very tailored lab coat, it is just the perfect color. It is really severe."

Chiren also visits the Kansas Bar, where the rough-hewn Hunter-Warriors hang out. For this sequence, Proctor relates, "All the Powers That Be really wanted her in a brocade dress. It's really hard to find good brocade. I did end up finding a great dress for that, but I had a white wool coat that went over that, so she really stands out at this bar."

# CHIREN'S LAB

Like her ex, Dyson Ido, Chiren works on cyborgs. Unlike Ido, Chiren works for profit in a state of the art facility, enhancing and repairing elite Motorball players, as well as the tormented Grewishka. "Think of it as the Mercedes-Benz of surgical," says art director A. Todd Holland. "It was no holds barred, top of the line, everything you could ask for."

"Chiren is employed by Vector, who runs the Motorball games," production designer Steve Joyner explains. "He's got unlimited money. This is what's happened after Chiren and Ido broke up. To show the contrast between the two, we definitely wanted to go ultra-sleek and high-tech."

Production designer Caylah Eddleblute describes the clinic's stainless steel and concrete look as "Brutalism meets deco. Everything surrounding Chiren, including Vector's environment, we worked hard to [make] cold, hard surfaces. She's in a loveless situation, she knows it.

There's no compassion in anything around her setting or environment. She's given that all up for something that she thinks will be better. We wanted a visual means to show she's now in this machine world, and basically sold her soul for it. It's an antiseptic environment. She works on research, development and repair."

Holland thinks that Chiren's surgical set is probably the most faithful to the early, 2005 *Alita* concept art. "The original concept, though very loose, had

**BELOW & OPPOSITE TOP:** Concept art of Chiren's lab, with Grewishka.

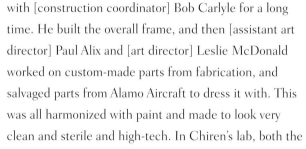

something that we all liked. Everybody reacted favorably to it. Steve, Caylah, myself, Robert Rodriguez, other illustrators, set designers – no one [felt] like we had to go in a different direction. I think the 2016 illustrators did another pass at it and fleshed out a couple more of the details, and then I gave it to our set designers, who really fleshed out the surgical area."

Chiren uses an outsized surgical frame to work on the hulking Grewishka. "The surgical frame was quite a build," Joyner recalls. "Production designer Walter Schneider carefully deconstructed the concept art and produced working drawings for construction. The large parts were actually cut by construction foreman Clete Cetrone, a wonderful pattern maker who worked

with [construction coordinator] Bob Carlyle for a long time. He built the overall frame, and then [assistant art director] Paul Alix and [art director] Leslie McDonald worked on custom-made parts from fabrication, and salvaged parts from Alamo Aircraft to dress it with. This was all harmonized with paint and made to look very clean and sterile and high-tech. In Chiren's lab, both the

**BELOW:** Early (2005) concept art of Chiren's lab.

**BELOW:** Chiren's lab set.

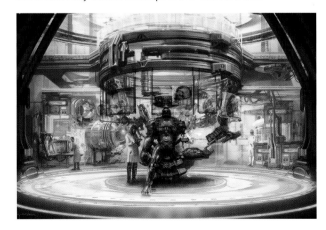

stair and the floor all have built-in LED lighting, and it is all a cool temperature to add to the coldness of the environment."

The lab set epitomizes the collaboration on *Alita*. "[Producer] Jon Landau would come in," Holland says, "we'd incorporate his ideas, Bill Pope, our DP, lit it beautifully, I used some ideas that I developed years ago for fun on a side project. Then Steve came up with this great automatic computer system in the background that would move on camera and do a certain little detail in the back, and worked on that with Richard Hollander, our VFX supervisor. That was the final touch."

Joyner says that everyone appreciated producer Landau's input. "I spent eight months sitting in his chair at Lightstorm during the development phase. Jon checked on the artists every day. He had a lot to say, and he is a good shepherd of art. He makes the process enjoyable for the artists, he's very creatively involved, and he's very hands-on in the pre-conceptualization of the work. He also was heavily involved with the editing of the [concept] reel that eventually won us the [greenlight for the] movie at Fox. A lot of that came from Jon's meticulous attention to detail. He was very thoroughly involved in the art, in a very good way."

**BELOW:** Concept art of Chiren's lab.
**RIGHT:** Costume design for Chiren
**FAR RIGHT:** Concept art of Chiren's lab, with Grewishka.

142

# HUGO

During the course of the film, Alita falls in love with Hugo, an ambitious Iron City street kid who plays street Motorball, rides a cool gyro cycle – and harbors the dark secret that he's a jacker who steals cyborg parts from their living owners and sells them on the black market.

James Cameron describes Hugo as someone who "aspires to go to Zalem by hook or by crook. He's a dreamer. I think we can all relate to somebody that wants to follow their dreams."

"Casting the role of Hugo was a little tricky," says producer Jon Landau. "There were a number of actors that we looked at and looked at and looked at. The difficulty is finding young talent that can hold the screen, that can both play the edge and the sensitivity that the character required. We did a number of screen tests. We just wanted to find the right actor. We looked at some 'name' actors. They just weren't the right mix, the right chemistry with Rosa [Salazar] for this. We felt that Keean Johnson was definitely the right choice. Not only is he right for Hugo, but I think he's going to be a star."

Character designer Joe Pepe, who worked on Hugo's look, empathizes with aspects of

**BELOW:** Concept art of Hugo.
**RIGHT:** Hugo (Keean Johnson).

**THIS PAGE:** Concept art of Hugo with Alita.

the character. "I own a motorcycle, so I know the feeling of riding along the beach with the wind in your face," he says. "There's a freedom to that."

Pepe remembers doing multiple hair designs for Hugo, digitally manipulating various coifs on a photo of Johnson so that the actor wouldn't have to submit to actual multiple haircuts. "[Production designer] Steve Joyner had taken several photos of him in a motorcycle jacket, and

sent those over. So I put that through over forty-some hair designs that took him from shaved, to dyed-his-hair punk hairstyles, to long hairstyles, braided, so they could see a photo-realistic version of the haircut."

Hugo's ultimate hairstyle called for a bandanna. "We went through quite a process of finding the perfect bandanna," says costume designer Nina Proctor. "He doesn't wear a helmet on his cycle. The bandanna is

to help keep the hair [out of his face] when he rides. Because it's around his face, that was the most important thing. We went with a dark navy blue bandanna that is really faded. Instead of it being a full bandanna, I cut it in half, so it was one triangle, and then rolled and tied it, just so it wouldn't be so thick and heavy on his head. Robert is very hands-on and he was very hands-on with that – he's a bandanna guy, so you can't fool him!"

**ABOVE:** Hair style variant concepts for Hugo.
**RIGHT:** Photo of Hugo's paralyzer bolt.
**FAR RIGHT:** Concept art of Hugo with Alita on his gyrobike.

For the rest of Hugo's look, Proctor continues, "He doesn't have a lot of clothes. All he is trying to do is save his money so he can leave Iron City and go to Zalem. So I didn't want him to have a lot of different clothes. There are a lot of longer-style T-shirts. Hugo is a bit like a rock star. His jacket is important. I probably tried fifteen jackets on him. I had this really aged leather jacket that had been made from really old leather pieces, a heavy-duty zipper in the front and with a lot of hardware, big clips that closed old army bags from World War II that went all the way down the back."

Hugo's pants, Proctor says, "Are more fitted, aged-looking jeans. He has some really cool, heavy-looking boots that are actually a really lightweight boot, army-style, lace-up, functional."

Hugo's jacker look required more pieces. "All along, I was trying not to have too many clothes in his closet," Proctor notes. "I added a second jacket that was in the same family as the [first], made from really old leather. But it has a hood on it, so he can cover his head that way, and then I found these really cool

goggles, and then he has the bandanna that goes over his face. I changed the bandanna up, not the one that we see him in all the time, but a darker bandanna that covers his face, and fingerless gloves, so you can't really see his hands. So there is a darker heaviness to him."

Toward the end of the film, Hugo is almost killed. Ido saves him by putting him into a Total Replacement cyber body. Concept artist Jonathan Bach, who worked on the design, says, "It's supposed to be a bit of a disappointment when Hugo sees his body, so it's put together from many different pieces. It's totally mismatched. Initially, we started with stuff that kind of felt like a Ken doll, like a mannequin. I didn't put those parts everywhere. I put them in the chest and the leg and the arm at first. Then it changed over to a little more mixed metal. Initially, I was trying to make it look poorly designed, or more generic prosthetics, so nothing special and nothing cool-looking, but just mechanical actuators and pieced-out parts from a mannequin, so it wasn't very impressive to look at. The chest was more mechanical."

**ABOVE:** Hugo wakes up after the Total Replacement operation.

Director Robert Rodriguez says for him the most challenging aspect of making *Alita* had nothing to do with the technical elements, but rather getting the emotions and the characters right. This was especially true in the climactic scene with Alita and Hugo, which he rewrote with James Cameron. "The motivation for Hugo climbing up [the supply tube] had to be different. In the manga, Hugo was like, 'Oh, well, now I can just climb up to Zalem and bye Alita, whether you want to go or not.' We lost respect for him. So Jim and I considered how we could keep that set piece, which was really cool, being on that supply tube, halfway between Heaven and Hell, and have it all work. I wanted to try to make it work with the iconography of the manga that Jim was inspired by, but we had to make it work dramatically. Having those conversations with Jim – my favorites were when we'd sit around and try and pound this thing out. It was great."

**THIS IMAGE:** Concept art of Hugo dying in Alita's arms.

**RIGHT & OPPOSITE BOTTOM RIGHT:** Concept art of Hugo in his cyborg body

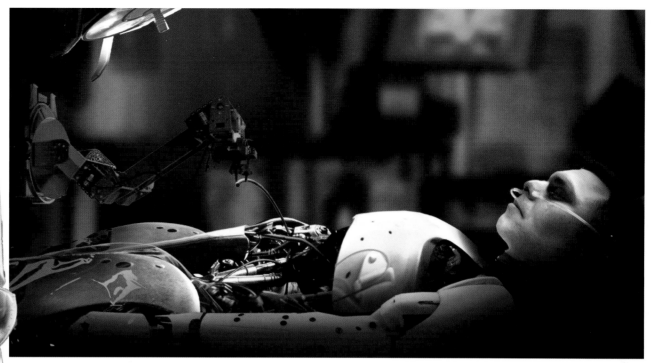

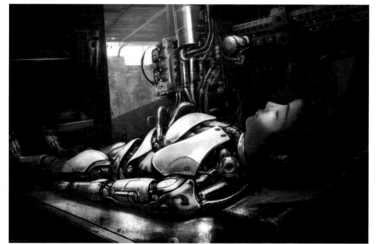

**ABOVE & BELOW LEFT:** Concept art of Hugo's cyber core being placed into his Total Replacement cyborg body, including early (2005) concept art (below left).

# HUGO'S GYROBIKE

Hugo and his friend Tanji both ride gyrobikes, a motorcycle-like mode of transport popular in Iron City.

Concept artist Jonathan Bach explains the gyrobike "is a single wheel rather than two. It operates with a gyroscope, so it doesn't fall over when you're riding it." A gyroscope is an apparatus consisting of a rotating wheel mounted in such a way that its axis can turn freely in certain or all directions, which is capable of maintaining the same absolute direction in spite of movements of the mountings and surrounding parts. "If you slow down, it'll hold balance on its own. There are some prototypes in real life, but they're not great-looking, because you're sitting on top of the wheel. On a normal motorcycle, your crotch height is going to be right about the wheel height. If it's there, you don't have clearance over the larger gyroscope wheel. We wanted to make the wheel larger to make the bike look better."

The concept "started with a couple designs in a few different directions," Bach recalls. "One was lighter and more nimble, and the other was more of a bruiser, very imposing, because at the time, we didn't know exactly how the Hugo character was supposed to read on screen. I tried a few different things and we iterated from this more rectilinear brutish design to something

**BELOW:** Concept art of Hugo's gyrobike.
**BELOW RIGHT:** Behind-the-scenes photo of Keean Johnson sitting on the on-set prop gyrobike.

**RIGHT:** Concept art of Hugo's gyrobike.
**OPPOSITE BOTTOM LEFT:** Photo of the on-set prop gyrobike under construction.
**OPPOSITE BOTTOM RIGHT:** Decals for Hugo's gyrobike.

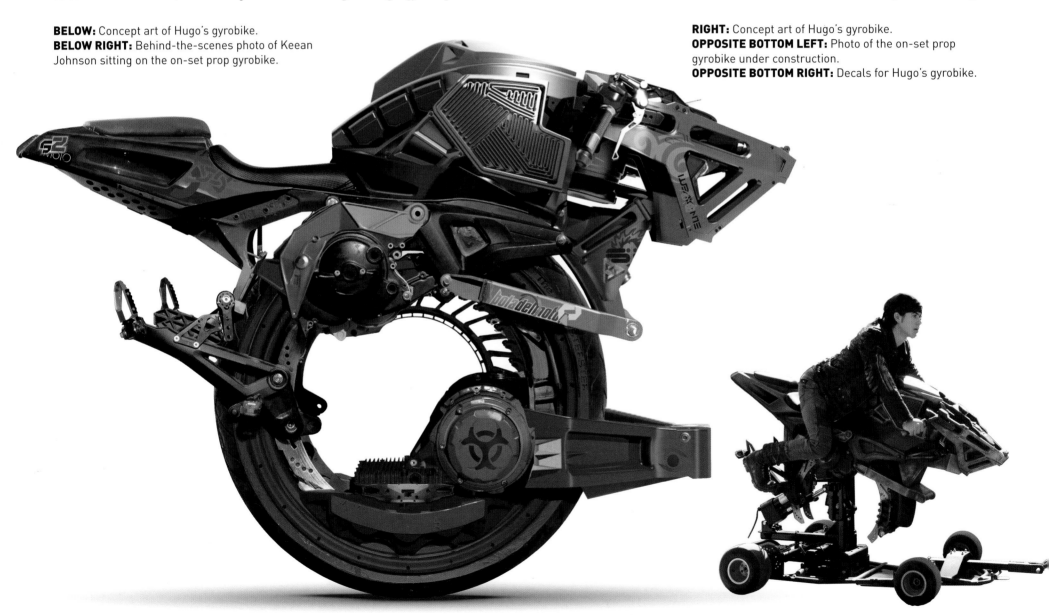

that was more sport bike-like in a modern way. That was a little two-dimensional. We probably went through a good ten designs before we modeled it in 3D and figured out its proportions and how a rider would actually get on, sit on and operate the bike."

Bach credits fellow artist Joe Hera with working on the design and translating it from 2D to 3D. "We used a little bit of inspiration from a well-known Italian motorcycle model, but we ended up going a very different way for the front end. The new direction was more skeletal. For this design, it was a line sketch to start, and then we used a lot of photos of parts of existing bikes. We looked at various different types of motorcycles. I started grabbing pieces, looking for mechanical forms I could play with to put together to make a finished silhouette."

Hugo's gyrobike has a sporty look, "more of a speed racer than a cruiser," says production designer Steve Joyner. "It can cut in and out, quickly maneuver, be almost a getaway vehicle. The Italian design influenced the place of the seat, the position of the handlebars. In our first iteration, the whole thing was a full-sized bike at PBE. We put two people on the bike and saw how they could sit comfortably and move realistically.

From that, we built a second bike that was spot-on. Fortunately, we had that large fabrication department at PBE available, where we could make full-size mockups, the producers and the director could look at them and decide how to shoot this for CG."

Tanji's gyrobike, Bach explains, "began as a design for Hugo. We went a different direction [for Hugo], but we wanted to take that design to Tanji. It was a little more elongated and pretty large when we actually put a human on it, so we chopped it and made it a little more bulldog in nature, but it retains the underside, the front-end farings of a modern motorcycle, and that makes it a little different. The head of the bike is a lot stubbier. It doesn't have a big futuristic shape up front, like [Hugo's] bike does. It looks like it's pieced together from many things, which is what we were going for, because these are all vehicles that are put together from scraps that fall from the city above."

Joyner admits with a laugh that at first he didn't think a gyrobike would work. "Jon Landau had a lot of fun proving me wrong," he says. "We found a guy who was developing a real working gyro motorcycle, and now we have real working gyro motorcycles in the background. The difference is, the practical ones are much smaller, so our heroes ride souped-up versions. That comes completely from the original manga. We came up with a full-sized mockup based on our initial concept. That first mockup became a background gyrobike, but it was really helpful to have that, because we could identify what worked and what didn't. We didn't want it to look like anything else, and when you have something supported on one wheel, you tend to tread in [other sci-fi movie] territory, and we didn't want that."

"The bike was also ergonomic," adds production designer Caylah Eddleblute. "You can have two people on a gyrobike. So how do you do that and have it look balanced, cohesive, not be overly bulky, and have it be able to have an element that can work on the set? We went through a series of iterations. The final version, the guys over at Lightstorm had particular points of view, and we incorporated them. Jon Landau cared about it very much."

"We wanted a hubless wheel," says Joyner. "The tire and wheel frame are integrated so that the drive system grabs the wheel inside the housing of the vehicle. There's no chain, there's no motor in the center – the motor is actually up in the vehicle's body, and that hubless wheel is a reality. There are hubless-wheel motorcycles out there. We just took it one step further and made it a gyro-balanced single-wheel motorcycle."

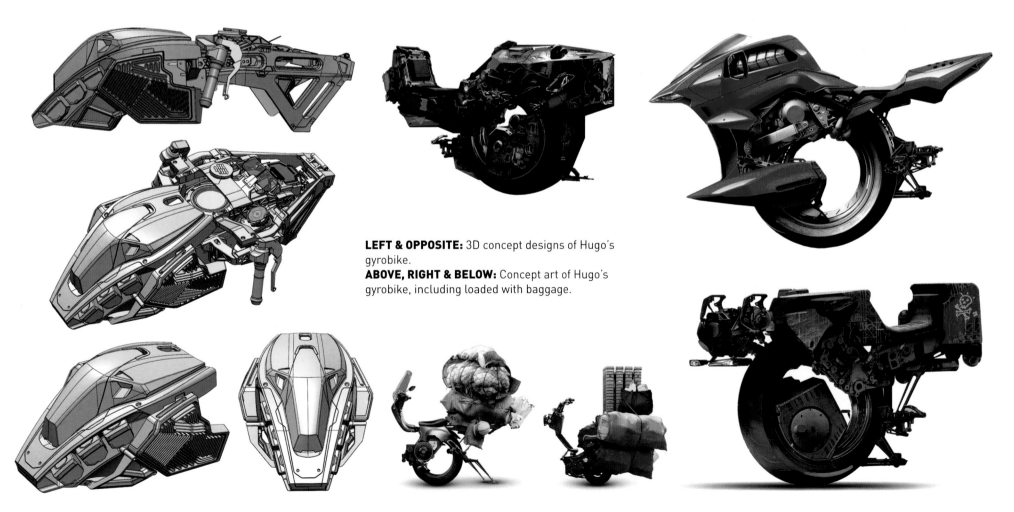

**LEFT & OPPOSITE:** 3D concept designs of Hugo's gyrobike.
**ABOVE, RIGHT & BELOW:** Concept art of Hugo's gyrobike, including loaded with baggage.

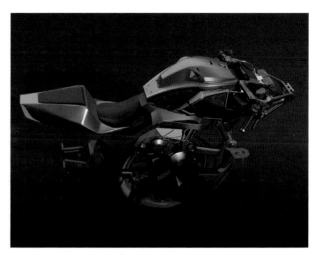
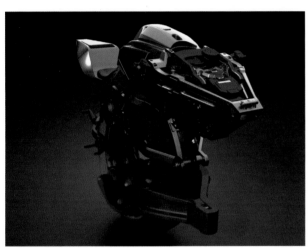

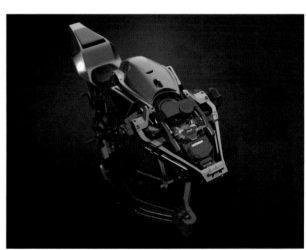

HUGO GYROBIKE
RADIATOR AND BATTERY ASSEMBLY
v01: WITH WEAR

JONATHAN BACH    09.21.16

# CATHEDRAL

Production designer Steve Joyner describes the ruined cathedral as "a relic from the colonial times of Iron City. It's fallen into disrepair and nobody really goes there. It's one of the places where Hugo takes Alita to give her a view of the city and Zalem, where Alita begins to realize that there might be more to life than meets the eye."

"I researched old cathedrals in Mexico City, and all over Latin America, and found some references with a decayed structure that was very Latin-influenced," concept artist Steve Messing says. "I did a lot of the aerial [views] of the bell tower, aerials of the kids. There was a rotten, collapsed roof. There are a couple of early illustrations – I can't remember who did them, years ago – where there was a balance to some of that decayed, collapsed look with what was still remaining and what it would look like. [The producers] were happy with the general vibe of that. We just made it more specific. I

**ABOVE:** Concept art of the cathedral at night.
**RIGHT:** Early (2005) concept art of the cathedral.

looked at cathedrals under construction to see how the bracing would work. There are World War II bombed-out reference photos, and we looked at a bunch of that, but there's also looking at how cathedrals were built. The arching forms, the crenellations on the sides, the way that the towers have these bell forms at the top that taper and flare, the columns, it's very specific."

Art director A. Todd Holland says of the cathedral, "We wanted it very practical. We built it on the back lot, two sides to three sides, steps in front, back, up the tower. It wasn't a full set. It needed to be incorporated with the back lot, and we also had rolling scenery. Sometimes we didn't want to see it, so we'd roll in a truck that would have another building [attached to it], so it would look like something else was back there. It is very much an old-school type of colonial stone church, based on many different things we found in Colombia and Europe and different [places]. Greg Papalia, our lead set designer, developed his own architectural language, based on all sorts of influences that we presented [to] him."

Though stained glass windows are a feature of most cathedrals, Holland points out there are none in the *Alita* version. "Glass wouldn't survive. There is wrought iron, there's statuary, there's carvings in the stone work."

The cathedral roof is meant to be 150 feet in the air, but in reality, "it was only, say, four feet off the ground,"

**BELOW:** Concept art of the cathedral.

Holland reveals. "So if [actors or production personnel] fell, they were only falling two feet onto a two-foot stunt pad. We constructed the roof set in a separate set on stage, on its own rolling platform that we could roll in front of the greenscreen."

Production designer Caylah Eddleblute elaborates that the cathedral roof set "was high enough that the camera could be low to shoot up at them, and then be able to get behind them and look down. That was built at Austin Studios, next door [to Troublemaker Studios]."

The cathedral is also meant to evoke certain emotions. "There was this beautiful decay," Messing notes. "We have these warm sunset moments, when Hugo and Alita are on the top of the tower. Their lives are this struggle in this slum, but there's a lot of beauty and moments that are found in a lot of these illustrations, whether they're in the market, or traveling around. So that moment, the way they're shot, they're framed with all this beautiful warm light, casting across the cathedral, and you see the two figures falling in love."

**RIGHT:** Concept art of the cathedral.
**ABOVE & BELOW:** Early (2005) concept art of the cathedral.

# KOYOMI

Koyomi is one of Hugo's street Motorball-playing friends. She is also Alita's first female friend who's about the same age, someone Alita can emulate.

"Koyomi was fun," says costume designer Nina Proctor. "We made her cute as a button. For her skate look, I used a lot of bright orange, but bright orange that had been taken down a tad by over-dyeing them and taking a little of the blackness out of them, but definitely orange. The kids are playing Motorball, imitating their favorite players. So she has her little T-shirt on. It was a baseball T. We hand-painted her numbers. Her favorite Motorballer is Jashugan. Even as [a cyborg], he is kind of dreamy looking, so of course the young girl goes for Jashugan. She has some braids that were woven into her hair that are different colors, and that play with the costume. Just cute, trendy styles."

# TANJI

Tanji is Hugo's friend, fellow street Motorball player – and cohort in "jacking," stealing parts from living cyborgs.

Hugo and his crew don't want to be recognized when they go out to "jack" (hijack) cyborgs and steal their body parts, so they therefore dress for anonymity. "It isn't like they have a uniform," says costume designer Nina Proctor, "but they are very covered. Each one has some kind of wrap that covers their head and face. They wear these big goggles, which were a collaboration between props and the costume department. They are covered from head to toe, including gloves. The gloves serve a practical purpose, too, because they're stealing these heavy metal pieces off of these cyborg bodies, so they need the gloves to handle these pieces.

"For Tanji's jacker look, I custom-made this long hooded sweater that was not made out of sweater fabric but out of a knit, with this cool hood," Proctor recalls.

"He is a bit more colorful than Hugo in his street look," Proctor continues. "The actor Jorge Lendeborg, Jr. is very lean, so he could do skinny pants, but just below the knee, with a longer T-shirt. He had this scarf piece that I made him out of a loosely woven fabric that I had dyed and aged. It was basically just a rag that he found. He had a couple different versions of that look, but it all looked like it came from within the same closet."

**FAR RIGHT:** Koyomi (Lana Condor).
**RIGHT:** Tanji (Jorge Lendeborg, Jr.) in his full jacker outfit.
**ABOVE:** Photo of Tanji's jacker crowbar.

**LEFT:** Tanji.
**ABOVE:** Concept art of Tanji's gyrobike.

# VEHICLES

There are many types of vehicles in Iron City, but all must be able to navigate its slim roadways. "One of the mandates from Jim Cameron and [producer] Jon Landau, also illustrated in the early concepts from 2005, was that, because Iron City has grown up so high, and been retrofitted so much, the streets are very narrow," explains production designer Steve Joyner. "To carry the biggest amount of people and/or goods, the vehicles have evolved into being thin and tall. We looked at reference from all over the world, from Korea, from the Philippines, things like tuk tuks and Kei trucks from Japan, all very small, efficient vehicles that can maneuver in these tight spaces.

"One of the first photo-bashes we did was with a local concept artist in Austin, Ted Bearzgon. [Production designer] Caylah [Eddleblute] and I pulled a bunch of photos of vehicles. Ted took them into Photoshop, then SketchUp, modeled them, stretched them, made them taller, and threw out a menu of vehicles that we could choose from," Joyner says. "From there, we went to concept artist Robert Simons with those sketches from Photoshop mock-ups, and he sat down and did some beautiful concept paintings. Working with them was so rewarding. The first artwork I got back was a gyro-truck. It was dead-on right."

Another early vehicle designs was for the yellow cab that drops off a young woman late at night, who is then attacked by Grewishka. "I gave Jeff Poss [who previously ran the Troublemaker fabrication department and now has his own company, PBE Exhibits] the painting of the yellow cab and said, 'Can you make me a mockup of this vehicle?'" Joyner continues. "In a couple weeks, he gave me a video of himself holding up the painting, which was printed on an eight-and-a-half-by-eleven-inch photograph. He lowered the painting and the exact replica of an operating vehicle was behind it."

Within the *Alita* story, all vehicles are electric, Joyner explains. "We don't make a big deal out of combustion

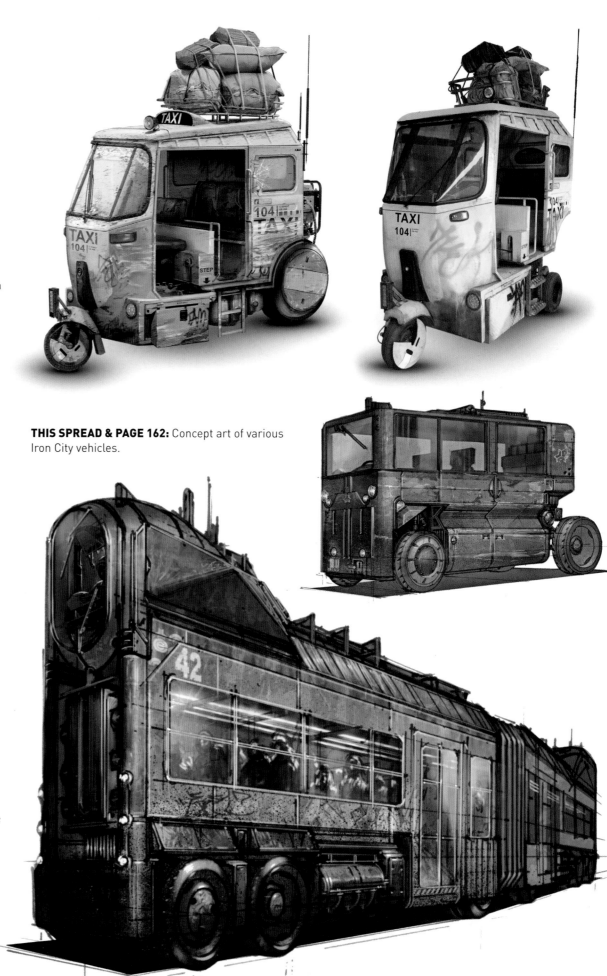

**THIS SPREAD & PAGE 162:** Concept art of various Iron City vehicles.

engines, gas tanks, things like that. All of the vehicles run on two big capacitors."

To manufacture the vehicles, the *Alita* production team turned to Poss, who had a team during production to build all the vehicles. "One shop was for building the bikes, one shop was for building the vehicles. We interfaced with them almost every day," says Eddleblute. "They were right around the corner. There were a lot of changes made once we had a prototype done – you realize there are things that work and don't work."

Practical versions of the gyro-truck were manufactured. On screen, "It runs on one or two wheels, it balances itself. In reality, it's a three-wheeled vehicle that stands up," Joyner reveals. "When we see the vehicle wide enough, Weta digitally replaces

the bottom of the vehicle with the gyro drive. One of the criteria that Robert [Rodriguez] had was, 'I don't want it to look like a golf cart on the street.' So we said, 'This thing needs to go forty miles an hour.' They found a motor and battery company that would allow the vehicle to do that. We had to put a stunt driver in it, because it could easily get out of control."

Eddleblute adds, "We also had on set, all the time, two crew members from PBE to man the vehicles, to move them into position, make sure they were safe, deal with any mechanical issues that might come up. They knew the vehicles, inside and out."

Although the production team had originally thought they'd have to paint over the vehicles so they could look like other trucks or cars in different scenes, "It turned out that we didn't need to," Joyner states. "We had built enough vehicles to cover the scenes. Each vehicle had its own design and its own personality, and the final concept art was developed by going back and forth with Robert Simons, and then working with Jeff Poss and the fabrication crew to get the vehicles built."

# CHOP VAN

One of the hero vehicles, the "chop" van used by Hugo and his jacker crew, "was a futuristic design that started with us and [concept artist] Ted Bearzgon," production designer Steve Joyner says, "and was brought to beautiful reality by [concept artist] Robert Simons. That van was custom-built out of sheet metal and classic panels that were CNC cut from the ground up. It's got a Tesla motor and battery in it."

**LEFT:** Concept art of the chop van.
**BELOW:** The chop van.

0561510001 僅限商用

90087

**ABOVE:** Decals for the chop van.

**RIGHT:** 3D concept designs of the Victory Gate.

**MAIN IMAGE:** Concept art of the Victory Gate and Hydrowall.

# VICTORY GATE & HYDROWALL

"The Victory Gate is the entrance in to and out of the city," production designer Steve Joyner explains. "That was one of the first things we shot. Caylah and the locations [department] found this picture of a great Brutal [architecture style] dam. That became the inspiration for the Victory Gate."

Production designer Caylah Eddleblute adds, "There were a lot of iterations of the concept art."

"The dam image really pulled it together, though," Joyner continues. "We only [practically] built a small piece of the Victory Gate. It went up twenty-five feet. We used a bluescreen and extras and vehicles coming in,

and the actual practical chop van driving out."

The Hydrowall in which the Victory Gate stands – an electrified barrier of high-pressure water 100 feet high which surrounds Iron City – also went through a number of different designs. "They changed it a couple of times," concept artist Steve Messing recalls. The concept artists

had to consider: "How much of the structure is visible and what does it look like? Is it like Niagara Falls when you're way up above it? How thick is it? It involved a lot of trying to create an image with all these components, but not having them compete and having just enough of them so that you feel like you understand what you're looking at, which was hard."

**ABOVE, BELOW & RIGHT:** Concept art of the Victory Gate and Hydrowall.

**ABOVE:** Early (2005) concept art of the Victory Gate and Hydrowall.

**ABOVE:** Victory Gate filming set.

# BADLANDS

The Badlands lie beyond Iron City. Alita, Hugo and their friends travel there, passing mechanical harvesters. "The mechanical harvesters are probably 150 feet long," production designer Steve Joyner relates, "and completely realized in CGI from a great painting by [visual consultant] Dylan Cole."

In the Badlands is the group's destination and an astonishing secret: a cratered lake containing a crashed URM spaceship, left over from the war. "The Badlands was shot on location here in Austin," says Joyner, "then extended in CG. We covered all the actors at practical locations and Krause Springs and McKinney Falls. The crater is McKinney Falls, but it's greatly expanded in CG. Weta is taking that and running with it, and that's based on another couple of beautiful concept paintings by Dylan Cole."

Weta visual effects supervisor Eric Saindon explains, "We've taken artwork that we received and added onto it to make it look like a rainforest in South America, and to be a bit of a crater with the ship stuck into it."

Besides the lake, "There are a few [practical] sections where they walk up this little path, and through some trees," Saindon adds, "that we were able to shoot on set. But everything else is just CG elements. We've added birds to try to bring the forest to life, to bring that little bit of nature to it. We always try to add bugs and things like that, so even if the viewer doesn't notice them, they'll sense something moving around."

**THIS IMAGE & RIGHT:** Concept art of the Badlands.

BELOW: Early (2005) concept art of the Badlands.

# URM WARSHIP

Producer Jon Landau points out that, while "I think we've held true to a lot of the manga elements, there are some things that are new. The idea of the URM is a totally new element."

The URM, or United Republic of Mars, battled the forces of Earth 300 years before the movie begins and the divide between the planet's surface and Zalem occurred during that war. Hugo takes Alita into the Badlands to show her a crashed URM warship, which she is able to gain entry to. Inside, she finds a Berserker suit. Ultimately, she realizes that at her core, she is in fact an URM Berserker herself, created for warfare. Despite this, Alita remains determined to forge her own destiny.

Visual consultant Dylan Cole did key art of the URM warship resting in a lake. Cole indicates a piece of artwork: "This is actually one of the first paintings I did, one of my favorites. When I did this, I didn't really have a conception for the design of the ship yet. I blocked together and kit-bashed a quick 3D model that I rendered and did a big paint-over to get this whole overgrown, ancient, crashed, eroded ship that Alita swims under and walks up through. She's super-heavy, and so she walks along the bottom [of the lake] and sees these giant engines and eroded metal and then moves forward

**THIS SPREAD:** Concept art of the crashed URM warship exterior.

**THIS SPREAD:** Concept art of URM warships during the flashback combat.

to a different part of the ship into a big gash. We were trying to figure out this whole sequence."

Citing another artwork, Cole explains, "This is a later view of the same thing from above, [as if] on a wide-angle lens." The artwork is more of a match to the Texas location where the practical background was shot. "This one is more like how they wanted to reveal it, from the lip of the crater, peering down into it."

Having designed the crash site, "Robert liked it, and then I had to figure out what the whole ship looked like," Cole recalls. "I had bashed together a rough 3D model, just to sell what this thing is and the idea was to have it be a classic science-fiction ship, where it's advanced, but it's not wholly unrelatable. It's not crazy, wacky alien technology, it's just more advanced technology."

During the movie, URM and Earth forces are shown in combat on the moon in a flashback. Cole also did key art for this sequence. For the front of one craft, "I was going for a nice hammerhead look, something aggressive and strong." The different engine ports, Cole relates,

"are for slowing descent and fine-tuning of direction as you are descending. Typical [movie spaceship] engines just propel the ship forward, but if you're being practical about how you land and maneuver, you need some counter-thrusters, so each one of those little thrusters is like an eyeball on a pivot, so you can do fine little adjustments to it."

Cole points out the drop ships bringing in fresh troops: "I'm thinking of it like an open space jeep. It's a little personnel carrier."

When asked what takes priority in spaceship design, how it works or how it looks, Cole responds, "Usually a bit of both. You want to come up with a shape that's cohesive and that's a statement, and then you reverse-engineer all the functionality, but before you even start, you need to know what the function of the ship is. For the URM ship, it started with that rear view of those engines in the crash site. I wanted a cool look at the back end of this thing – I wanted big engines, a big shape jutting out and shapes I could punch holes in

**THIS SPREAD:** Concept art of Alita approaching the URM warship underwater (left), entering the ship and passing through the fight deck (below left) and finding the Berserker body.

graphically, to show the erosion of it. And a slight anime feel, a slight nod to the source material. It's something that is kind of aggressive and cool, and feels advanced but relatable. A bit of a juggling act!"

Inside the crashed URM ship, the empty Berserker form is protected. "There's an energy field in the armory, protecting the Berserker body," Cole explains. "It's an intact body, which is why it's being protected. It's the most valuable thing [on the ship]. Where you see that clean sphere, it was perfectly clean inside of that force field, then Alita deactivates it and you see the difference [between that area and] a couple hundred years of moss and algae growth.

"We started with a grander room," Cole continues, "but over the course of working on the design for the interior and going over it with Jim, he wanted it to feel like much more of a practical, functional ship. It's not like a luxurious yacht. All the rooms are only as big as they need to be. There are lots of bulkheads and wires and pipes and all that stuff going through it."

Much of the final URM spacecraft design came from James Cameron. "We took all his designs and built it [in the computer]," says Weta visual effects supervisor Eric Saindon. "We went out and shot some photos of old, rusty tanks and some worn-out metal that we used for textures on the ship, but the design is so unique that

we had to build it from scratch." The same is true of the thrusters. "They're never on when it's crashed," Saindon adds, "so they're just big empty metal tubes."

The command deck and armory of the URM ship are completely CG. "They're all based on artwork from the art directors," Saindon states. "We have also tried to take ideas from other Jim Cameron movies, like *Aliens* ship designs, even *Abyss*, because it's supposed to be a bit of a cargo ship, but using the concepts that the [*Alita*] art directors supplied."

**BELOW:** Concept art of Alita discovering the stasis sphere inside the crashed URM warship.

**THIS IMAGE:** Concept art of Alita finding the Berserker body.

# MOTORBALL

Before they could fully realize the Motorball track for the film, someone had to figure out the sport itself. "There was a bunch of wonderful concept art images by the Lightstorm art department, and then I took those images and developed the larger track," recalls art director A. Todd Holland. "But Motorball in the comic was largely undefined. It was people running around, skating around, chasing a motorball. It was very difficult to discern, what are the rules? How do you score? How many people are out there? To design the track, I thought it was important to learn the rules. So I sat down and conceived some rules, took little bits of this, little bits of that, put them all together and sent them out to [production designers] Steve Joyner and Caylah Eddleblute and [producer] Jon Landau to get their feedback. In my first concept of Motorball, Jon Landau singled out the goal-scoring element, whether it was

in a hoop or a net, and he felt that was too much like [other sci-fi movie sports]. So I came up with an idea that, instead of scoring, it's more a game of possession. You have the motorball and complete a circuit on the track, and that's how you score points. If you have the ball, obviously, people are trying to get that ball from you. Then I made an entire document with officials, track specifications, what the play is, and so on. Then I designed the Motorball track."

Holland also thought there should be different kinds of Motorball games. "European soccer leagues have basic league games. Within that, they have different cup competitions, different tournaments, and there are different styles, different formats, whether they're single knockout or round-robin tournaments," he explains. "So in Motorball, I thought you could have team competitions, cutthroat competitions, or even just all-out chaos [with]

no teams at all; it's every man for himself. I thought of every which way a stadium promoter and a Motorball promoter could get [fans] in the seats."

To play Motorball, it's necessary to have a motorball. But, given the sport's importance in the *Alita* manga, it was surprisingly hard to find an image showing how the ball worked, Steve Joyner recalls. "Caylah and I found one image in the eighteen manga books, in one of the little three-inch by three-inch panels, that showed a cutaway of a motorball as part of the backstory. We keyed on that. I sat down with Paul Alix, one of our assistant art directors, who did the background and 3D printing, and we spent twelve days printing and painting and putting the parts together, and it turned out far better than I'd expected."

This was before *Alita* was even greenlit. "It's a pre-pitch piece of physical concept art, but it says, 'This is

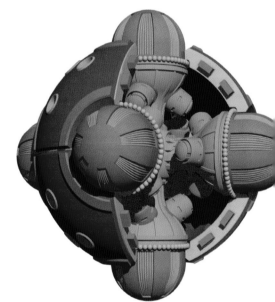

**LEFT & ABOVE:** Photos of the motorball prop.
**ABOVE RIGHT:** 3D model with cutaway of the motorball.

the language of the movie,'" Joyner adds.

The motorball prop was one of the biggest practical pieces made for the film. "Jim Cameron visited us during pre-pre-production and he held that motorball," says Caylah Eddleblute. "I think he had a lot of fun checking it out. The design comes right from the manga."

"The motorball is motorized – hence the name – designed in the game to move chaotically, to make it more challenging to capture and hold onto," Joyner explains. "It has various holes and mechanisms for gripping, and it's made out of armored plates, because it has to survive in this robotic arena. The wheels that stick out of it are steel as well. It's a heavy object, [forty kilograms or] about ninety pounds in story mode. It's a very dangerous sport for humans to play."

The motorball also has protrusions. In the CG version, "Those bend and project, go in and out, rotate, and make the ball move randomly down the track,"

Joyner continues. "So it's not like a rolling ball, where you can kind of get an eye-line and know it's going to go a certain way. This thing may take a left turn unexpectedly and everyone may crash."

The on-set version "is made out of 3D printed plastic," says Joyner. "We have one that's painted photo-realistically. It looks like armored metal, almost like it's made out of one-inch-thick tank armor."

"The motorball in the Alita manga is thirty centimeters [or 11.8 inches] in diameter and weighs forty kilograms," Holland says. On set, "We had different motorballs for different aspects, but all the manga size," Todd continues. "Some were rubberized, so we could throw them around and it wouldn't hurt anybody; some were kind of weighty, like in the manga. We had more of a hero, camera-ready version, but if you're throwing the motorball around, you want something a lot lighter-weight for the actors."

As a financial backer of the sport, Vector has a lot of Motorball championship trophies. The trophy was designed by Holland, who explains, "We wanted detail on the skybox shelves, and it made sense that Vector would have his team's trophies. I talked with one of the heads of the prop fabrication department and she sketched something homaging the FIFA soccer trophy, which was perfect." The base branches out into "two forks. It's got a little swoop, like it's flying down the track, and the motorball is on top, a gold and silver motif."

**BELOW:** Concept art of Alita's Motorball tryout.

**RIGHT:** Photo of one of the Motorball championship trophies.

# MOTORBALL STADIUM

With a film as reliant on concept art, CG and VFX as *Alita*, pre-production, production and post-production merge to an extent. Director Robert Rodriguez cites the Motorball track as an example of this. "Because post is so much, 'Okay, we have place-holders for things that we shot,' we didn't have it completely visualized yet. What exactly does the Motorball track look like? We knew a couple of the sections that they go on for some key action, but what is the overall lighting and the materials? We had some indication of what it was going to look like, but we didn't nail down everything like we had to on the physical set."

Rodriguez looked forward to shooting Alita's Motorball sequence in particular. "Jim's description was so breathless, I was leaping out of my seat, because it's not that Alita's going to play the game – she thinks she is, but they've hired a bunch of killers to take her out," Rodriguez says. "So the stakes are Jim Cameron stakes, they're sky-high. You get a sense of what the game is through an earlier scene, but when this one starts, it's to the death. So it's about the speed – they go off at a

**THIS SPREAD:** Concept art of the Motorball stadium main entrance.

hundred miles an hour – she's trying to stay ahead of them, trying to use everything at her disposal to take them out and stay alive. If it's just people racing around, playing a game, then it's only so exciting. What Jim described is something else completely."

In *Spy Kids 3*, Rodriguez had staged the 3D Mega Race, which he loves. "I've seen people borrow from that a lot, because it has some cool things with a made up track, with gaps and jumps and crazy things. So I know that this speed in 3D works really well. [In *Spy Kids 3*], those were vehicles. [In *Alita*'s Motorball], we have people in there. There was nothing to shoot live action, except for the lineup, when they are about to start the race. The rest is CG. We have an animatic, but figuring out the exact lens, lens size, lighting, what's in the background at any particular time, that's almost like starting from scratch. We have something blocked in, but we're able to go,

'That's what we had blocked in, but now that I see the CG track, why don't we put the camera over here?' Then you can start fine-tuning it. It's exciting."

Production designer Steve Joyner also cites the Motorball sequences as an example of *Alita*'s collaborative process. "The character designs for the Motorball players came from these wonderful concept designers at Lightstorm. Working out the mechanics of the track and the track action came from the script, and making it in a design form came from the art department, specifically [art director] A. Todd Holland working on that beautiful SketchUp model. Then the beautiful rendering textures are produced by Weta, under the supervision of [producer] Jon Landau and Robert Rodriguez."

The Motorball stadium was designed to have multiple vantage points for the crowd. "It's more or less one track, but it can go way up to the top of the

stadium, and way down to the bowels. It ranges all over the place," visual consultant Dylan Cole observes. "In the interior of the stadium, we're trying to show how there was an industrial foundation to some of the structure. This might have been some refinery tower that they have built on to make viewing platforms. You want to challenge what a stadium is. Instead of a bunch of people sitting in a circle looking in the middle, we wanted to have people all over the place, less like a [sports] stadium and more like a rock concert, where there are large platforms that people sway. You've got Jumbotrons facing all directions, no guardrails. It's almost like a mosh pit, very interactive."

The track also offers choices to the players, Cole continues. "You can take the faster, albeit more dangerous route, or you can take the safer route. Previs did a bunch of wonderful stuff. A. Todd Holland

deserves a lot of credit for reconciling so much of our disparate concept art and stadium build to come up with that cohesive track design. Obstacles exist on the course to impede movement and have people bash into."

The track's texture, "would probably be asphalt," Cole adds, "but we also wanted it [to look] like it's been run over a lot. So you see some crappy, corrugated metal there to patch it up and there'd be concrete, too."

Concept artist Jonathan Bach worked with a number of others on a particular shot of the Motorball track. "Crashed Ice is a real sport they play on rollerblades on an ice track. It looks vaguely similar to Motorball and we got a lot of inspiration from it," he explains. "That shot I worked on uses the idea of very steeply banked tracks, so that at the Paladins' high speed, running in these tight corners, it's about how the turns give them more track to run vertically up the side. In the illustration that I did, the upper half of the track where it banks is Plexiglass, so that you can see through if you're a spectator behind the track. We did undulations and track obstacles that can destroy a Motorballer's body, if they're not careful. Or they can use those details to shove an opponent into them. They would have to make quick decisions or hit something."

**TOP:** Concept art of the exterior of the Motorball stadium.
**ABOVE & RIGHT:** 3D models of the Motorball track layout.
**BELOW:** The official Motorball logo.

**ABOVE & BELOW:** Concept art of the Motorball stadium track during a game.
**LEFT:** Concept art of Alita and Hugo as Motorball fan spectators.

The color of the track sections depends largely upon the lighting, Bach says, "but it's characterized by really bright graphics that indicate where you are on the track. If you look at car race tracks, you'll see in the turns complimentary colors dash along there a bit more, so you have a really good idea of where the edge of the track is and how far you can take your car."

Holland worked on refining the track, which is just under two miles in length and 146 feet from the ground at its highest point. "It's concrete, with metal substructure," Holland says. "A lot of the banked curves have clear Lexan plastic, so you can be right underneath [the players] and see them go right by. I concentrated on the layout of the track, so as the players are speeding down, there's a left bank turn here, or a right bank, or a zigzag there, or the jump is here. We did not build any of the track practically, except for the pit area. Paladins came down the ramp into the pit area, and it's like a wagon wheel, and each spoke is a different team."

The pit is where the players and their color-coded crews prepare. "It's like a NASCAR pit," Cole explains. "This would be the base of one of those more industrial towers in the center. So you take an off-ramp to come down below." The pits are connected, with low barriers between them that allow each crew to see what the others are doing, and for the cameras to see them all at

**ABOVE:** Concept art of Motorball player banners for the pits.
**BELOW, OPPOSITE BELOW & FAR RIGHT:** Concept art of the Motorball pits.

LEFT: Concept art of pit maintenance cranes.

once. "Each one of these banners is showing the stall or the pit for each racer. It's a person not a car the crew is working on, so you want that proximity for the character fun and intimidation and trash-talking," he laughs.

The design team had fun building the Motorball crew pits. "The SketchUp model that A. Todd Holland did visualized the track for us in preproduction," Joyner says. "From there, we realized [the pits are] a cross between a pit stop and a medical bay. We needed racks that would support these large players and lift them up for servicing, and then the set decorators stepped in and introduced all the tools and ladders and fueling hoses

and mechanics' equipment that each of the teams would use to service their players and then Nina Proctor came up with these beautiful costumes for the pit crews that identified each individual bay and player within a pit crew. So again, we took that from Formula One racing."

"We built three pit bays, and then digital effects could expand out in the wide shots," production designer Caylah Eddleblute explains. "But we had enough space so we could get the skaters to come in, and still accommodate the intimate moments between Vector and Chiren, and Hugo and Alita, while they're interacting."

Joyner adds that another consideration was having

enough room "to get a camera far enough back for the right perspective so that the live-action set could be dropped into this CG Motorball track."

The stands were also shot as live action. "We used a stadium here in Austin that is made of concrete and has beautiful aging and weathering," Joyner states. "We dressed and adapted that. The two or three hundred extras that we had, dressed up and rooting for their team, were watching a blue screen. The art department designed the high-tech vendors in the crowd. When a vendor makes a motion of pouring or dispensing, even though the pack they're wearing may

**THIS PAGE:** Concept art of Motorball player maintenance equipment in the pits.

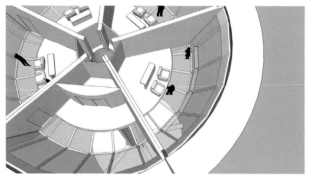

**LEFT:** Concept art of Vector in the skybox.
**ABOVE:** 3D set designs for the skybox.

be this unusual, high-tech-looking thing, the audience gets it. Jason Hammond, our property master, created these beautiful backpacks."

The stadium also has a locker room, which was shot practically in a separate building near the studio. Eddleblute recalls with a chuckle, "The room was absolutely grim, unattractive, full of gunk and one of those wonderful challenges when you have to see what you're made of and how much can your imagination create."

"We did use some of the existing grime in there," Joyner says. "It had been a service bay for trucks, I think. We had to get rid of some of the textures in there that were wrong, though. It looked a little like a trailer house exploded."

"Jeff Adams, one of our set designers, worked so that it felt like the underneath of the Motorball stadium," Eddleblute continues. "He built a ceiling piece that

was accordioned to feel like there was stadium seating above. We brought in fixtures, we did graphics work with [graphic designer] Ellen Lampl's great eye. We also brought in our tunnel pieces that were modified from another project, so we had a curved set piece where the actors could roll in and out, apparently to the Motorball stadium. That set had to play two different locker rooms."

Joyner adds, "Dave Hack, our set decorator, found these wonderful steel shelves that they then modified as benches for the cyborgs. Construction was disposing of some of their used table saws. They had flashes that looked great in lighting, so we had [paint supervisor] Mike Mikita paint them in a metallic color and then stacked them on the wall…"

"And created a completely different look," Eddleblute finishes.

Vector's section of the stadium skybox was also built

practically. "Vector has the best view in the house," Holland notes.

"The skybox set is a work of art," Joyner says. "Storyboard artist Marc Baird worked on that with A. Todd for quite a while. It follows the architecture from [Vector's] penthouse. This was an elevated set that was up in the air about twelve feet. The first four feet of it were a glass floor. As you walked in, it felt like you were going to drop right through. The first AD kept asking the weight load of the floor. He was worried about falling through the glass! Dave Hack brought in a wonderful modern bar, and then we built some lit alcoves that he dressed with trophies and artifacts. Jennifer [Connelly] brought her young daughter to the set. She was mesmerized by the glowing prop artifacts and fell in love with these two lighted bookends, so we sent them home with her."

# MOTORBALL PLAYERS

Visual consultant Ben Procter explains that in Iron City, "The Motorballers are celebrities. They're known by name. A Motorballer is a combination between a Formula One driver and an NBA superstar. These guys are up there as gladiators, ripping one another apart. Half the kids in Iron City want to be these guys one day. The fact that you've got beat-up ones that are your Oxycontin-addicted ex-football player, and the size of them, is in part where you get your criminal class of Iron City. The pro ballers are the current ones that have funding, like an actively supported Formula One program. There's R&D [research and development] going into the parts. Then you've got the castaways, the freak show of former Motorballers, who are using their own money to keep themselves running these overwrought bodies that were never meant for the streets."

The pro Motorballers are known as Paladins; some of the less successful players are on the Factory team and moonlight as assassins or Hunter-Warriors. "I think the Paladins share a sleekness. They have money and sponsors," concept artist Fausto De Martini says. "Some of the armor they wear is more designed, fit to the body. The thug Motorballers, they're more like, 'Okay, I'm going to find a part like this.' So they are much more hacked together."

The Motorballers "are all new concepts," De Martini says. "We saw some of the anime designs, but we wanted

**BELOW:** Concept art of Motorball Paladin Whipcopter.

**BELOW:** Whipcopter movement function sketches.

**BELOW:** Concept art of Motorball players chasing Alita.

to do something that was a little more extreme than those. It was cool, because we had a lot of freedom. There were quite a lot of artists involved in this project, and quite a lot of designs that were made in 2005 that carried over as well."

Weta senior visual effects supervisor Joe Letteri says a lot of what differentiates one Motorball player from another "is really done in silhouette. You're looking for a way to make each one look distinct. This is not a cookie-cutter world." For the ex-pros, "They're in a way the dregs and they have to make their pieces almost uniquely. At one time, there might have been standardization, but over the years, they've had to cobble things together. So that gives us the ability to make each one unique."

Concept artist John Park designed several Motorballers and supplied the 3D artists with imagery. "I work predominantly in Photoshop in 2D, so I was tasked to come up with ideas to help pass that off to a 3D designer or modeler to fully flesh it out for CG," Park says. "It's a combination of using a lot of photo references and a lot of painting digitally to get the right concept." For some Motorball players, Park used sections of motorcycles, "a combination of Triumph bikes and a lot of different types of speeder bikes."

"In certain cases," reveals Procter, "the very large cyborgs are turbine-powered, so the guy who has a jet engine, he's using it not so much to propel himself as to generate power. That could be an old Lear jet engine or something like that. Other stuff could be repurposed from old cars. Some of the guys have very deliberate panels, like dragster cars, or exhaust pipes coming out from the engines on their backs and stuff like that. So there definitely could be a car element. The high-end Motorball racers are human Formula One cars, MotoGP bikes. The punkier characters might borrow a little more from the Harley [motorcycle]."

In filmmaking terms, "hero" doesn't necessarily mean good guy, but rather the version of who or what on screen is the focus of a particular shot. "Pretty much all the Motorballers have to be hero," explains Weta visual effects supervisor Eric Saindon, "because they're all individual builds, and we see them all fairly close. Some of them don't actually have actors playing them, but we have to use an actual head and put it inside of these guys, so we put a generic head in the ones where you don't actually see their face, and put it on a hero body."

However, for the Paladins, "we've got actors for most all of them," Saindon elaborates, "and then we've taken that actor's proportions – head, arm length, leg length, that type of thing – and pushed them into a CG character. We're

**LEFT:** Concept art of Alita on the starting lineup at her Motorball tryouts.
**RIGHT:** Concept art of a Motorball Paladin.

not trying to keep them the same size, but we try to keep the same proportions, so that when they're moving around, when they swing their arm, we get that motion, and we can put that back in our CG Paladin, so we get the performance the actor did on our CG versions."

With all the Paladins, Saindon continues, "We build a first [3D CG] version, so that people can see it rotating, and then we can do motion capture. Some of the Paladins looked cool in the first designs, but as soon as we started to move them, they didn't work. So we have to put them through motion tests with our animators to make sure they can bend their arms, they can skate, they can do all the things they have to do, and then when we show that back to Lightstorm and Robert, if everyone's still happy with it, we go in and start adding the higher-end detail to the design, like how a helmet opens, how his head attaches to his CG body; how all the different elements of the different characters come together to work with their designs. We block out their basic idea, like them racing around the track, and then we go back and we decide things like, 'Here we want this guy to do something cool, so we'll have him spray out fire,' or any number of other things."

In the final version, "The pro players are all completely digital characters," says Letteri, "so once we're into the Motorball scene, everything [Paladins and Factory players] is completely digital. We shot some close-ups for some of the actors, so we use real actors' faces in a couple of shots, but once we get into the action scenes, they're all digital."

To inject a spectrum of color into the Motorball players, Procter says, "I think that's where the Factory aesthetic came into it. Those guys that have mechanical arms, they're bright yellow or bright red. The cybernetics can be brightly colored. In certain cases, we tried to have people adorn themselves, almost like self-graffiting, because all of these parts are not brand-new, so they might do a home repaint of it, and why not go colorful with it when you do that? I think part of it is a collage aesthetic. If you have to jerry-rig a piece of mechanics or even your body together with all this different stuff, you're naturally going to get a diversity of materials, of colors, that you wouldn't have if they were custom-made or right off of an assembly line.

"There are people who do artwork where they literally go get old car parts out of junkyards and assemble them into beautiful art," Procter adds. "We looked at art like that and said, 'What does it look like when you take a whole bunch of things that aren't meant to go together and slam them together?' We had to walk a line between a patched-together, lovingly restored Havana aesthetic, and something that still looks like it's in our future."

**LEFT:** Concept art of Motorball Paladin Claymore in action.
**RIGHT:** Concept art of Motorball Factory player Gangsta.

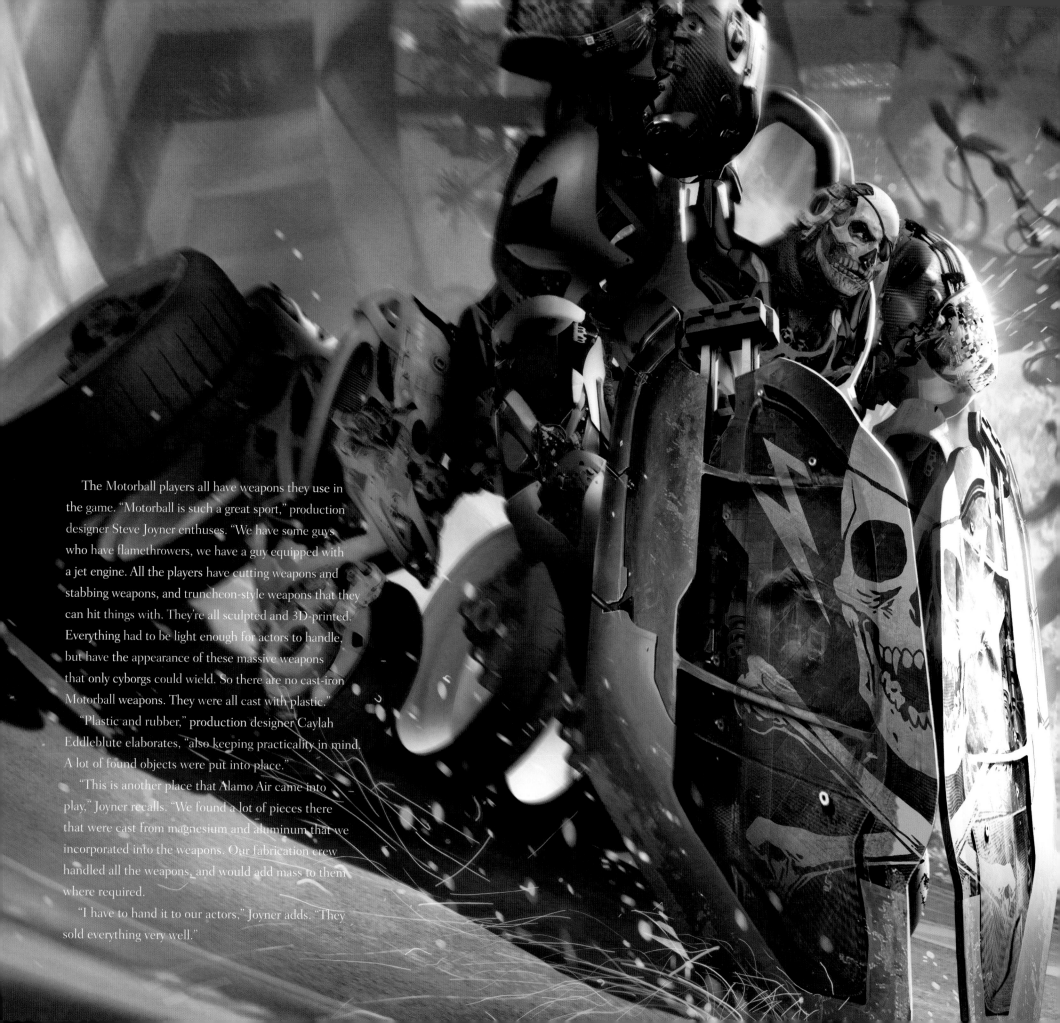

The Motorball players all have weapons they use in the game. "Motorball is such a great sport," production designer Steve Joyner enthuses. "We have some guys who have flamethrowers, we have a guy equipped with a jet engine. All the players have cutting weapons and stabbing weapons, and truncheon-style weapons that they can hit things with. They're all sculpted and 3D-printed. Everything had to be light enough for actors to handle, but have the appearance of these massive weapons that only cyborgs could wield. So there are no cast-iron Motorball weapons. They were all cast with plastic."

"Plastic and rubber," production designer Caylah Eddleblute elaborates, "also keeping practicality in mind. A lot of found objects were put into place."

"This is another place that Alamo Air came into play," Joyner recalls. "We found a lot of pieces there that were cast from magnesium and aluminum that we incorporated into the weapons. Our fabrication crew handled all the weapons, and would add mass to them where required.

"I have to hand it to our actors," Joyner adds. "They sold everything very well."

**LEFT & BELOW:** Concept art of Motorball Paladin Skaramasakus.

**ABOVE:** Concept art of Motorball Factory player Gangsta.
**BELOW:** Early (2005) concept art of a Motorball Paladin.

# JASHUGAN

Concept artist Fausto De Martini relates that champion Paladin Jashugan was one of the pro Motorball players originally designed back in 2005. "Jashugan was really cool, he was really well done originally, so when we came to this project later, we decided to keep that [character design]."

De Martini's own work on Jashugan, he says, was specifically for the shot of him in the pit, "where you can see his exposed torso and things like that. We created that in order to show the studio that this was a more realistic take on *Alita*."

**BELOW:** Concept art of Jashugan.
**RIGHT & OPPOSITE TOP:** Concept art of Jashugan's helmet removal stages.

**BELOW:** Early (2005) concept art of Jashugan.

# AJAKUTTY

Like most Motorballers, the Paladin Ajakutty has two bodies: one for the track and a more human look when he's out on the street.

For the latter, "We gave Ajakutty a sports look," costume designer Nina Proctor says. "He is very active, he gets in a bar fight, he does all these incredible moves. I had worked with the actor [Marko Zaror] before, and he does these kick-boxing moves. I knew that Robert wanted him to be able to do these really incredible kicks, and so I had to make sure that his pants were functional. So they are a stretch fabric. And then a sports jacket I customized with embroidery showing his Motorball number. It gave him the future-jock look. I kept it within the colors of his Motorball body, red and black."

**LEFT:** Weta Digital original 3D model of Ajakutty.
**BELOW LEFT:** Ajakutty (Marko Zaror) in his street clothes.
**BELOW:** Concept art of Ajakutty.

# CRIMSON WIND

A pro Motorball player, Crimson Wind is smaller and faster than most of the Paladins, built like a speed skater. She is number 7.

**THIS PAGE:** Concept art of Crimson Wind.

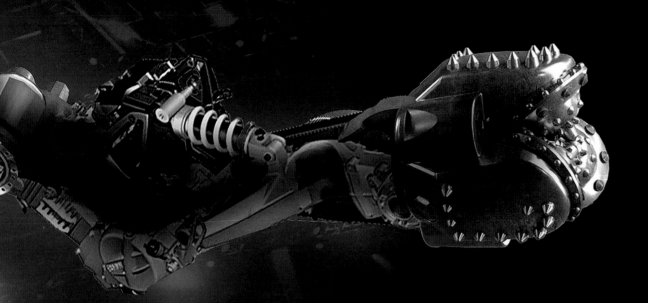

# JUGGERNAUT

Concept artist Fausto De Martini worked on the Paladin Juggernaut, number 14. "We were trying to figure out the look of the bad guys who go up against Alita, so we came up with the concept that some of the Motorballers are not bipedal and they have wheels for legs. This guy has three wheels, and he has a big gorilla arm and three others, and the shot that I did shows him extending the big arm and yelling. He's like a UFC fighter, so I used that kind of facial expression in the artwork, like he's someone spoiling for a fight. I felt it was a cool touch. For all his mechanical parts, I used parts of cars, engine blocks and air intakes, to express the idea that, even though it is a character, it is a character that is designed to race like a vehicle.

"Because he's a tough guy, I looked for parts that are bold, because a lot of cars nowadays tend to be a little sleeker, even in the engine parts," De Martini continues. "You might say these are cars from the 1980s or '90s, a little more muscle car. He has a visor, where it can come up and down, because whenever they're racing, they need to have some sort of protection on the face. He also has a mechanical Mohawk, so he looks like he has a Mohawk, but it's actually plating in the head. He only has a very small section of the face showing, everything else is machinery."

Juggernaut also has a drill weapon as part of one of his other arms. "I went online and looked for different types of drills and found this really interesting-looking drill bit that is used on really hard rocks," De Martini relates. "It has little diamond bits and it's like three drills together. I made it much smaller for Juggernaut, because I had to fit it in his hand. I did a quick model in 3D, because I needed to pose the whole character, and then that's what I ended up using as his character reference."

**LEFT:** Concept art of Juggernaut.
**ABOVE:** 3D model concepts of Juggernaut.

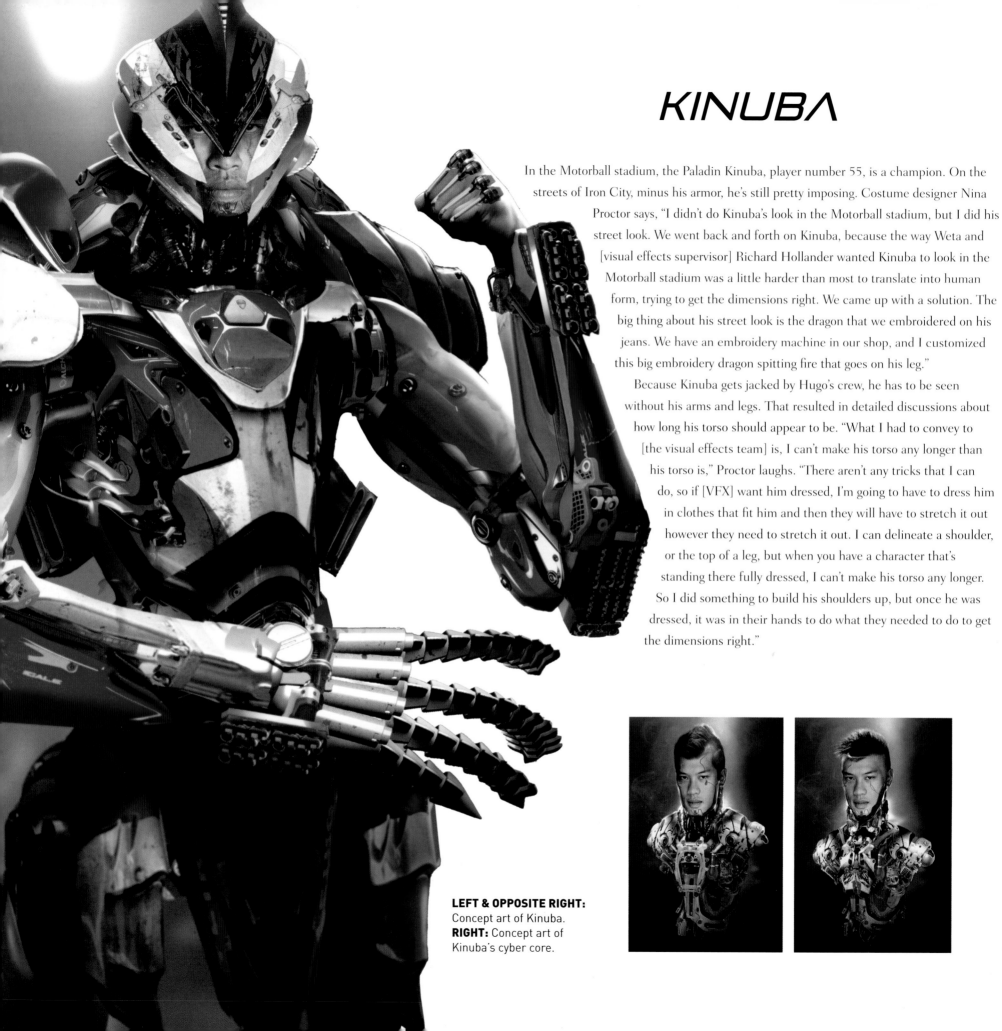

# KINUBA

In the Motorball stadium, the Paladin Kinuba, player number 55, is a champion. On the streets of Iron City, minus his armor, he's still pretty imposing. Costume designer Nina Proctor says, "I didn't do Kinuba's look in the Motorball stadium, but I did his street look. We went back and forth on Kinuba, because the way Weta and [visual effects supervisor] Richard Hollander wanted Kinuba to look in the Motorball stadium was a little harder than most to translate into human form, trying to get the dimensions right. We came up with a solution. The big thing about his street look is the dragon that we embroidered on his jeans. We have an embroidery machine in our shop, and I customized this big embroidery dragon spitting fire that goes on his leg."

Because Kinuba gets jacked by Hugo's crew, he has to be seen without his arms and legs. That resulted in detailed discussions about how long his torso should appear to be. "What I had to convey to [the visual effects team] is, I can't make his torso any longer than his torso is," Proctor laughs. "There aren't any tricks that I can do, so if [VFX] want him dressed, I'm going to have to dress him in clothes that fit him and then they will have to stretch it out however they need to stretch it out. I can delineate a shoulder, or the top of a leg, but when you have a character that's standing there fully dressed, I can't make his torso any longer. So I did something to build his shoulders up, but once he was dressed, it was in their hands to do what they needed to do to get the dimensions right."

**LEFT & OPPOSITE RIGHT:** Concept art of Kinuba. **RIGHT:** Concept art of Kinuba's cyber core.

**ABOVE:** Concept art of Kinuba in his street body and clothes.
**BELOW:** Concept art of Kinuba's head and neck.

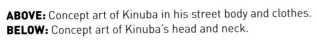

# ZARIKI

Concept artist Fausto De Martini worked on the quadruped Paladin Zariki, player number 38.

"He looks like a race car, because of the shape of the body," De Martini says of Zariki. "He has four wheels and instead of having his body up vertically he has a longer torso with his head up front. So whenever he runs, he looks more like a car, [running] on all fours. He has the arms in the back [of the torso] to carry the ball, because it's part of the game. He can use the arms for grasping, but he also has big, sword-looking attachments on them. He's all blue, he looks like a Formula One car, with an air intake on the top of his head. The idea on that was, we have the Paladins that look a lot like a human, bipedal, upright, and I thought that it would be cool to go the other way, horizontally, where he looks a lot like a vehicle. He has a little head, but it's clear he looks like a vehicle with a head in it. I thought that it was cool to have the full range of the character."

**OPPOSITE:** Concept art of Zariki.
**RIGHT:** 3D model concepts of Zariki.
**BOTTOM LEFT:** Early Weta Digital model of Zariki.

# CLAYMORE

The Paladin Claymore is more human-looking than many of his peers. "He has a suit of armor," says concept artist Fausto De Martini, "kind of like a medieval knight. Not every Paladin has to look like a sleek Formula One car. We were trying to vary some of the designs, so that was a lot of fun. Luckily, when Jim [Cameron] saw this guy, he was pleased."

"Claymore wears chainmail," costume designer Nina Proctor says of the character requirements for shooting. "They had to have the chainmail piece that fits on his head, and just the very front of his face shows. There's chainmail starting at the chin and then it goes around the neck and down onto the chest a little bit, over the shoulders. That was really all I had to do for Claymore. He primarily wore the grey [performance-capture] suit, but they really needed that physical part of the chainmail."

**LEFT:** Concept art of Claymore.
**ABOVE:** 3D model concepts of Claymore.

# WINGMAN

Wingman One and Wingman Two are near-identical Factory Motorball players. "We wanted them to appear to be twins," says costume designer Nina Proctor. "In their Motorball bodies, one [Wingman Two] is red and one [Wingman One] is blue, so I did a play on that [for their street look] and dressed them in red and blue, and gave them a jock look. These characters are the pro football players of the day. So I threw in some of the sports world."

# EXPLODER

Exploder is one of the Factory team players sent to assassinate Alita on the Motorball track. Visual consultant Ben Procter describes him as a TR, or Total Replacement, "a guy who's a head on a stalk, he's kind of got a jet engine attached to what would be his left shoulder. He's basically a vehicle."

"Exploder is on two big wheels, and he has a fireball-shooting thing stuck on the side of him. It's in between a flamethrower and a missile launcher," Weta visual effects supervisor Eric Saindon elaborates. "It shoots fireballs of sorts. You're not actually supposed to have projectiles in Iron City, but he's a rebel so he's bending the rules."

**ABOVE:** Concept art of Exploder.

**ABOVE:** Concept art of Wingman Two.
**RIGHT:** Concept art of Exploder in his street body and clothes, with his jet engine.
**BELOW:** Concept art of Exploder's jet engine.

**ABOVE:** Concept art of Gangsta.
**BELOW:** Concept art of Gangsta's head and neck.

**BELOW & OPPOSITE RIGHT:** Concept art of Gangsta in his street body.

ANTIOCH FACE STUDY

# GANGSTA

Weta visual effects supervisor Eric Saindon describes the Factory Motorball player Gangsta as "a mixture of a motorcycle and a human. He's down on all fours, with a really big tire in the back and two little tires on his forearms, and he's in a crouched position. He looks basically like a V-8 engine with a head stuck out of it."

"The character has tattoos all over the face and arms, but the entire body was replaced and he looks very specifically like a vehicle," says concept artist John Park, who worked on the concept art for Gangsta. "This character was intended to be a mercenary that tries to take down Alita, so one of the design prompts was to not only make the Motorballer a fierce racer, but to make him a lethal weapon. There are a lot of blades and some design accents that we needed to introduce to the

character, to make him look really menacing. We looked at a lot of industrial machinery and saws, things like that. A lot of what I referenced was junkyard tech, so things are welded, bolted down. Nothing is really refined in that sense. Everything is found objects that are attached and bolted on."

For Gangsta's built-in weaponry, Park adds, "The blades came from big band saws. The blades are attached onto the side of the arms, so that when he's racing on the track, he can bump into any character and cause a lot more damage than just bumping. The anatomy of the character is not humanlike. When you look at the silhouette, it looks very much like a human body and a motorcycle surgically melded together. That was the concept."

**LEFT:** Patrick Gathron in Gangsta makeup and full mocap suit, with two of his blades.

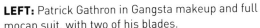

# STINGER

In Motorball mode, Factory player Stinger resembles a giant cybernetic scorpion as much as he does a man. Character designer Joe Pepe designed Stinger's street clothing and face. "I don't know how much of his face is actually visible," Pepe says. "It's just a portion of it, with these large blade-like features coming out of his jaw."

Another illustrator, Joe Peterson, worked on Stinger earlier. "Stinger started off with more of a military/militant-type look. He had one cybernetic arm, one human arm," Pepe recalls. "A lot of that came out. [Visual consultant] Ben Procter wanted to mix things up, so that not everybody had the same basic feel. I created a logo, like a bumblebee or a hornet, the whole stinger concept, that was put on his jacket."

Weta visual effects supervisor Eric Saindon notes that when the character is on the track, "Stinger has

two giant chainsaw blades for arms, and we're using those to basically cut through other characters. When they're at the starting line, we use some plates for the Motorballers, but for the most part, they are all CG."

Pepe observes of his fellow *Alita* artists, "Everybody has a different methodology. I work mainly two-dimensionally in Photoshop. A lot of the other artists will develop a 3D geometry in a simplified form, and then render that element and then paint on it in Photoshop. Jonathan Berube had created an entire 3D geometry of Stinger in his foundation [Motorball] concept design that was moved on into final development. I took his concepts and created Stinger's street body.

"They gave me his illustration of Stinger swinging his big segmented arms on the track, and blowing things up. Ben had said to just keep the element of his head, but put

it with a street look. So he's in a more humanoid body in the street look, with the cybernetic arm and the cybernetic enhancement to head and neck." Even in repose, Stinger is distinguished by his ferocious facial expression.

Costume designer Nina Proctor created some costuming for Stinger when he's in the locker room. "He is just a mess of things, found clothing and found pieces," she laughs. "It is a cool look, but very aged and rugged. He's on this team that is going up against Alita, the B team. They're very much mercenaries. I found an old army jacket that I customized into a piece – I took the sleeves out of it. It was an army coat that was heavy-duty felt, longer, probably at least below the knee. I did have these really cool gloves that he wears that go all the way up his right arm that we customized, just to give him a little more presence."

**BELOW:** Concept art of Stinger in action on the Motorball track.

**ABOVE LEFT:** Concept art of Stinger's street body head, shoulders and clothes.
**ABOVE & BELOW:** Concept art of Stinger.
**LEFT:** Photos of Stinger's street body head sculpt.

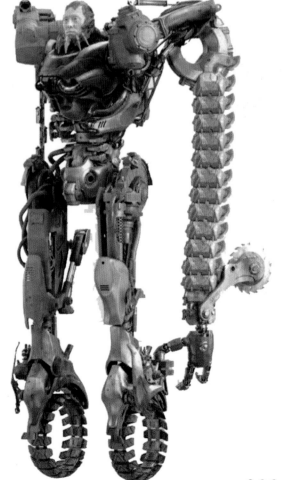

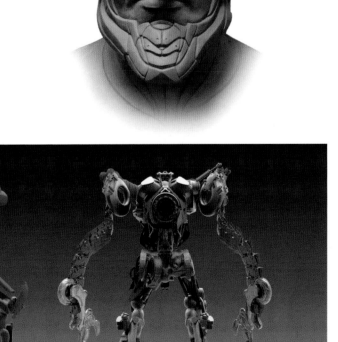

# MACE

Costume designer Nina Proctor says of Factory Motorball player Mace, named for his signature weapon, "He is just a rugged kind of character. For his street body look, he is a big guy in real life, and so I wanted to build on that and made him rough and tough, almost hood-like, because that's who these people are, mercenary types."

**CLOCKWISE FROM RIGHT:**
Concept art of Mace in his street body and clothes; 3D model of Mace's head; Concept art of Mace.

# KUMAZA

Factory Motorball player/assassin Kumaza, character designer Joe Pepe explains, was first conceived as a Hunter-Warrior. "[Visual consultant] Ben Procter had given us some room to develop some characters. Kumaza started off as a more refined bounty hunter, in the sense that I used a multi-million-dollar car interior to create pieces of Kumaza's body – it's got really high-end interior leather seating, multi-colored stitching, and then multi-colored leather on the seat and the interiors of the doors. I had taken elements of the seat and modified those.

"We ended up giving him some weapons," Pepe continues, "a type of [close-combat] knife called a karambit that has a loophole at the end of the handle, so you can spin it on your finger. He has six of those as abdominal muscles, in a sense, that cover his abs. They're pointed inwards. The way I had imagined it, he could grab them two at a time or one at a time, and it wouldn't disassemble his body in any way, it was just the location of where they were sheathed in the abdomen. And he has two large daggers in his thighs. Because his thighs are mechanical, they act as the sheaths for those blades."

As with several other Total Replacement cyborg characters in the film, the concept for Kumaza included the use of negative space. "There are openings in his chest and his shoulders and the side of his head, and then a lot in his legs, because his legs are all leather and metal framework," Pepe explains. "Then he has some fleshy parts with tattoos. Up his sternum to his neck

is flesh, and then the front part of his face is flesh. I roughed it out and Ben would come in and critique it."

Procter notes that Kumaza is one of numerous characters who treat cyber enhancement as "a form of fashion. Having people use skin, which is actually cyber skin, patterned on themselves in a way that is totally arbitrary and designed, and putting tattoos and other decorative aspects on that skin. If you're a cyborg, why would you always choose to look robotic with your robotic parts if you don't have to? Cyber skin looks great, and your face is cyber skin, so why wouldn't you extend that down? The Kumaza character has a chest that looks muscular. Are there muscles in it? No. But it looks cool and sexy, and he's got tattoos on it, and it ties it into his face."

It's important to vary where flesh meets technology, Procter adds, "because the risk with these characters is, if you just take the cyber core and the typical main parts of human anatomy, you start to get this kind of human head stuck onto a robot body thing. Or a human hand stuck onto a robot arm, where if you put the break line just where somebody's cuff would be, that's what it looks like, a hand coming out of a weird sleeve. So we tried to find cut lines for where the flesh goes that defy the typical breakdown of functional parts."

**ABOVE:** Photo of Kumaza's sword.
**RIGHT:** Concept art of Kumaza in his street body.

# SCREWHEAD

Although much of *Alita: Battle Angel* is based on the manga, some of its characters are original. Screwhead is one of them. "She started off as just a Hunter-Warrior that I had illustrated and Robert liked the design," character designer Joe Pepe says. "Initially she was an extra in the bar scene, and then became a Factory team Motorballer. So we developed her a bit further, with a street look and a Motorballer look. Screwhead got the name after the illustration. [Visual consultant] Ben Procter and I were looking at some engine part, and he said, 'That's a really cool shape, throw that on her forehead.' Then it was a matter of scaling the shape up and down until it worked. It was just what ended up looking the best to everybody."

For Screwhead's forehead piece, Pepe elaborates, "We had a lot of motorcycle photos: engines, farings, framework, frames, some independent pieces and some complete motorcycles. With the independent pieces, getting a different view or angle could show different elements to the design that you don't normally see on a completed motorcycle. It was an element of one of those that caught Ben's eye."

Since some concept artists have more expertise with human features and others specialize in mechanical designs, there were

**LEFT & RIGHT:** Concept art of Screwhead.
**ABOVE:** Concept art of Screwhead's head.
**OPPOSITE TOP LEFT & OPPOSITE RIGHT:** Concept art of Screwhead in her street body and clothes.

**LEFT:** Screwhead's street body hand tattoo.

frequent collaborations during the *Alita* design process. "If [concept artists] John Park or Jonathan Bach were more proficient at illustrating some of the hard-surface cyborgs, on some of them I would create the head and they would do the cybernetic body," Pepe explains. "On Screwhead, Jon Bach did the cybernetic arm and I did the humanoid head and her wardrobe. I started the illustration of her sitting at a bar with a cigar, then Jon Bach illustrated the cybernetic arm, then I finessed the arm with Ben [Procter].

"She is basically a human face with the jawline from the masticating muscle back as an open cage framework, so you can see the cybernetics from the side to the back of the head," Pepe continues. "Her right ear is separate from the side of her face as well. It's like an island on the side of her head. The right side of her face is all a cybernetic framework. Her forehead has the circular shape on the left side, just

below her hairline. Around that is cybernetic, metallic engine part-type material."

Negative space was also a consideration in the design. "A lot of it was in the neck, so that it didn't look human, and it didn't look like a human in a suit," Pepe explains. "It was one of the key factors, making sure that there was enough negative space that it didn't look like someone just wearing a prosthetic."

"She has a very feminine sort of design, a little bit more lacework in her metalwork. She's also got four arms and a thirty-foot chain," Weta visual effects supervisor Eric Saindon says dryly of Screwhead's Motorball body.

In order to properly animate Screwhead, Saindon continues, "We needed to mimic the look of a cyborg with four arms and creatures never would match up to that." So the inspiration for her movements came from machinery rather than a quadrupedal animal or an insect.

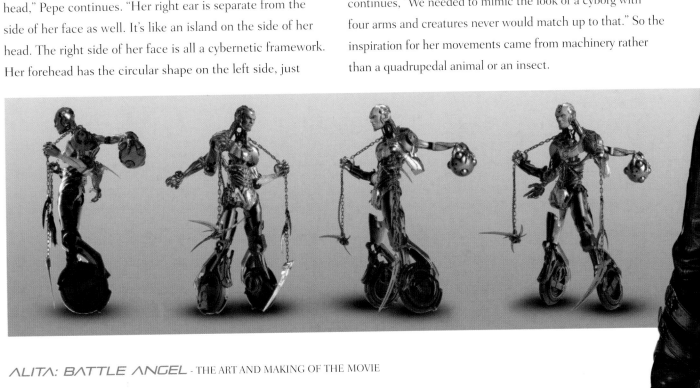

# GELDA

Played by Michelle Rodriguez, Gelda is an URM Berserker teacher who mentored Alita before she was "Alita."

"Gelda is a full CG character," explains Weta visual effects supervisor Eric Saindon. "The head is based on Michelle's body scan, with a different hairstyle from Michelle, with bigger eyes, smaller mouth, more swept-back hairstyle, but a similar body to [Berserker] Alita."

Character designer Joe Pepe worked on Gelda's look. "I did a lot of variations of her costume, as well as her portrait," Pepe recalls. "Initially, Robert [Rodriguez] picked a frame out of the manga that had her hairstyle and a pose. I did a photo-realistic version in the same vein and methodology as Alita – the bigger eyes, etc – but one of the Troublemaker artists had done a computer rendering of Gelda, so I used elements of her shiny face and the highlights on that and introduced that into my artwork. Then Michelle was cast and I was doing different sizes of her nose and her eyes and hairstyles. [Concept artist] Fausto [De Martini] rendered her costume. We settled on a concept art level, design-wise, and took that methodology and applied it to Michelle. But because her facial proportions are a little different [than those of Rosa Salazar], the percentages varied. We started with the same percentages, but then massaged it to make it look more like Michelle."

**LEFT & BELOW:** Concept art of Gelda.
**RIGHT:** 3D model concept of Gelda in an URM spacesuit.

# NOVA

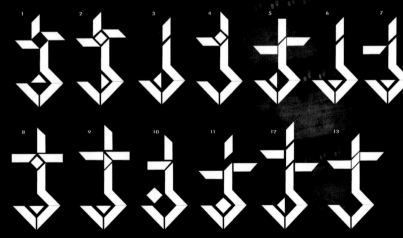

Nova is a mysterious figure who influences events in Iron City from his perch in Zalem above.

Character designer Joe Pepe worked on the design for Nova's costume. "I started with this pure white outfit. My inspiration was just the purity and the godlike status," Pepe explains.

"Then the design focused on the goggles. There were a couple of different shapes and designs," Pepe continues. "It was just the proportion, lenses and shape that covered more of his eyes and eye-socket area or less. Then a bunch of different lens designs, how much it came down over his cheekbones. A lot of the goggles ended up looking too bug-eyed. I even did one [pair] that was straight out of the manga. We also used elements from what the art department at Troublemaker had done."

There is also some CGI involved with Nova's goggles. "For the scene where he puts on glasses so that he can look at Alita down below in Iron City, the actor basically just makes the motion like he's putting on glasses and then we're putting CG glasses on his head that unfold onto his face," reveals Weta

visual effects supervisor Eric Saindon. "They're like a telescope."

Costume designer Nina Proctor says, "Nova is pretty special. We shot Nova about a month after we'd completed principal photography. I had made three choices for his main suit. One was a bit more simple-looking, although it was made out of satin, but it was important to Robert that the suit be able to move in the wind, so he chose a really lightweight fabric. The actor loved the way that suit looked, but it just didn't feel heavy enough. So I said, 'I just happen to have one more suit.' It was a three-piece suit. The actor fell in love with it, and I customized it to fit his body. It's silk in a lunar silver color, the color of the moon. It offered a little bit of weight. It's a longer-style coat with very slim-fitting pants. I made the shirt out of linen, but it has a silver thread woven into the fabric. The closures down the front aren't buttons, but a series of very delicate, beautiful chains. His suit is more 'futuristic' than most of the costumes in the movie. I wanted to make him a little different from anyone else."

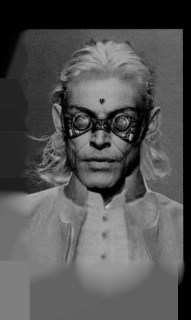

**FAR LEFT & ABOVE:** Concept art of Nova with his goggles.
**LEFT:** Concepts for the Mark of Zalem forehead tattoo.

# ZALEM

In *Alita: Battle Angel*, the floating city of Zalem hovers above Iron City, forever out of reach. Once connected to the surface by a space elevator, Zalem hasn't been accessible from the Earth for centuries, so few ordinary folks have any real idea what it is like.

Production designers Steve Joyner and Caylah Eddleblute concur that Zalem's look in the film is fairly true to the manga. "It was designed to have a sense of mystery, a sense of elegance, almost cathedral-like," Joyner says. "It's very futuristic and it's an extreme contrast to life below on the ground. It's not really translucent, but it's made up of a lightweight carbon nano-tube [designer and inventor] Buckminster Fuller-

type of structure. The architectural style is on the bottom and is modeled a little bit on the architect Zaha Hadid's work. What we tried to keep and the concept artists tried to communicate was an abalone/alabaster feel. It's got a depth to it, but it's definitely solid."

The audience briefly views Zalem obliquely from the side, but mostly as the Iron City denizens do, from below. Visual consultant Dylan Cole says, "It's almost a dual metaphor. We're living in the shadow of Zalem and feel the oppression of this. At the same time, it's also aspirational, so it's this glittering jewel in the sky. So it's oppressive by its shadow, but it still should be a thing of beauty, and we also want to show that this is from

**THIS SPREAD:** Concept art of Zalem.

a lost, more advanced era. That's why we had to have a lot more swoopy, art nouveau lines, compared to the brutality and the industrial nature of Iron City."

A long jagged shaft descends from the bottom of Zalem. "That is the broken shard of the bottom of the space elevator," Cole explains. "That used to connect down to Iron City, [before it] was blown up during the war. [Concept artist] Steve Messing did some initial work on the trumpet shape and the texture. I took it and did a whole pass putting this art nouveau paneling all over it, making it look a little more elegant."

A lot of different people had a hand in Zalem's look early in development, according to Messing. "I created some 3D models early on. I worked under Dylan. We did surfacing detail passes of the underbelly of the city.

The flavor of what that architecture ended up being, the flowing [architect Santiago] Calatrava influences, the graceful line work, those kinds of influences affected the form language of the belly of Zalem. We also looked at B-52 bomber schematics and got some texture maps from that and worked them to get a filigree of line work from the blueprints, and wrapped it over the geometry to the surfacing of the belly of Zalem."

These are the patterns seen on Zalem's underside. "Some are more subtle, some are bolder and more graphic," Messing says. "We did a lot of versions of, 'How dense is the detail? Is it thicker, is it thinner?' There are areas that have graphic negative shapes that punch into the surface, and then you get areas of lighter filigree that extends outward. It's a balancing act, a

dance between very graphic cutout shapes and elegant, tapering, flowing forms that have some level of fine filigree to them, but not too much."

Messing laughs when asked whether the shapes on Zalem's underside are meant to have function. "A lot of it was just purely graphic design," he explains, "but also trying to [emphasize] the contrast between the dystopian Iron City and the hierarchy of this richer, more affluent culture that literally looks down upon them, and showing the contrast between an elegant structure that was a little more graceful than the trash in the heap below it and the cluttered [Iron City] culture."

The design team was mindful of what Zalem would look like in frame with Iron City below it. Messing describes techniques that were used for this. "Some of

**BELOW:** Early (2005) concept art of the landscape before Zalem; Zalem as it was first built; and Zalem during the events of the film.

**TOP LEFT:** Early (2005) concept art of Zalem from below.

**ABOVE & BELOW:** Concept art of Zalem from below.

**ABOVE:** Concept art of the underside of Zalem.
**BELOW:** Concept art looking down on Zalem from above.

**LEFT:** Concept art of Zalem from the planet surface.    **ABOVE:** Concept art of a closeup section of Zalem at night.    **BELOW:** Concept art of Alita's final challenge to Nova.

those 360 spherical paintings, we would camera-match the set photography and then, in 3D graphics, we'd put a rough version of the 3D model of Zalem in there, in perspective, correctly, and try to frame it. Then we did visual effects paint-overs once we had plates that they actually filmed of the actors. We literally tried to match, in real-world scale, in the computer, to the plate photography, and position accurately what Zalem would be. So we knew in the framing what it would actually look like in the shots."

While Zalem is always overhead, we don't necessarily see it constantly, Messing notes. "There's an artistic quality that the narrative dictates that can override the technical aspect of Zalem in this frame. We'll take it out or shrink it, we'll cheat." This also applies to how much Zalem's position above factors into the lighting. "Zalem doesn't cast that crazy a shadow all the time."

# ZALEM SUPPLY TUBES

Supply tubes are one of the signature features of Iron City. These supply tubes are used to transport goods and products from Iron City to Zalem above.

Even the guide ropes attached to the tubes are enormous. "Those are probably thirty-five or forty feet in diameter," visual consultant Dylan Cole notes. "The footing for the guide rope is almost as tall as the Empire State Building. So it's larger than it appears. There is some access there, and there are actually defensive mechanisms on cables to prevent people from going up [to Zalem]."

The tubes are equipped with lethal sliding rings to stop anyone who dares to try to ascend. Concept artist Steve Messing explains, "There was some art direction on the tension cables that lead up to Zalem. Dylan did a ton on the braces, but we did a bunch of 3D models for the engraved, serrated [rings], the patina, and the inset grooves that wrap around them like a braid. We have shots right up on one of those things, so they can't just look cool from far away. It's got to make sense when we're right up on them."

Weta visual effects supervisor Eric Saindon provides further detail on the defense rings, which are entirely CG. "They're spiked donuts that fly down each tube and spin as they come down to make sure that no one climbs up. So they're basically a big circular blade that goes up and down the tubes to make sure they're clear."

"We conceived [the tubing] largely with the Lightstorm art department," art director A. Todd Holland explains, "and then our set designer developed it and came up with the size and shape and the detailing. But when it came down to building it practically, Robert only needed just a partial piece and used bluescreens and greenscreens. It was a twenty-four-by-thirty-foot cross-section of a forty-foot-diameter tube, and we could slant it different heights. We also had another part later on

**LEFT:** Concept art of a defense ring moving down a Zalem supply tube.
**RIGHT:** Concept art of a supply tube defense ring.

**ABOVE:** Early (2005) concept art of Hugo on a supply tube.

**ABOVE:** Concept art of a defense ring moving down a Zalem supply tube.

that was just so [the actors] could hang off it at the end, [made of] wood and plaster and metal. But the detailing of that would become completely computer-generated."

For the climactic sequence, production designer Steve Joyner reveals, "Practically, what we built for the actors to walk on was a curved set. We couldn't put them forty feet in the air. The correct radius was twenty feet wide and about thirty feet long, and tilted up at a fifteen-degree angle. It was painted grey and the performers [playing] Hugo and Alita wore performance-capture suits. So other than developing the textures and the overall scale and look of it in the concept art, the actual practical build was simply the section of that tube that they could perform on, and I think we shot on it for two days, getting all the action, which will all be enhanced by CG."

More work was required for the flashback firefight on the tubes. "We did designs of what the energy blasts would be – a lot of development went into the effects work on that as well," Messing explains. "We're trying to do something that we haven't done before. We don't want it to look like a fireball in [a] videogame, we don't want it to look like just beams of magic. We went for plasma trails that tapered out. There is a dissipating trail and a blue-turquoise tint to it."

Regarding the *Alita* designs overall, Cole explains. "It's different case by case. Usually one person works on a [concept art] image. Both [fellow visual consultant] Ben Procter and myself are illustrators and concept artists ourselves, but we're also art directing all the others as production designers. So Ben and I do a lot of the work ourselves, but also lead the team and offer direction to everybody.

"[The production design team] would get the brief from the script, and sometimes from Robert, but a lot of times, we would just take a crack at it ourselves, knowing what the needs of the story are," Cole continues. "For example, one particular piece was something that, just knowing that we had all these pipes and knowing that we have people living on multiple levels of this city, I was going to propose, 'Let's set a scene up here, walking on all of these pipes.' That way, it's not like, 'It's a weird, scary place to be,' it's just, 'Treat it like a street.' I would have discussions with [producer] Jon Landau and Robert about it, and we actually had a fair amount of freedom, which was a lot of fun."

The tubes running through Iron City also sport colorful graffiti art. "I definitely wanted that Aztec/Mayan/Latin American feel in there," Cole says. "I put that several places, and they had some wonderful graphic artists work on that for the set build. There's a strong tendency in a lot of science fiction to go very Asian with the influence, so it's fun to embrace all the Latin stuff."

**ABOVE:** Early (2005) concept art of the footing for a supply tube guide rope.

**RIGHT:** Concept art of the footing for a supply tube guide rope.

# CONCLUSION

For all the incredible creativity and hard work done by the designers, special effects artists and the production team, director Robert Rodriguez feels that what's most important about *Alita: Battle Angel* is camaraderie, story and character, as conceived by James Cameron. "That's the thing with Jim. It looked like it could have spectacle, but it's always going to come down to the story," Rodriguez says. "You can never judge a James Cameron movie just by its title or its one-sheet or its artwork. He does so much, he's so smart in that way, so creative, and will engineer a story that will really affect an audience. [Cutting the script down to feature length] was a joy. There was so much great stuff to work with. And that was the key, to keep what he would love and lose the rest, so that he didn't notice what was missing."

In fact, the heart of the film is "literally Alita's heart," Rodriguez adds. "It's what gives Alita her personality and her life. She's born into this world with such optimism, and her viewpoint is so different. She's seeing everything with fresh eyes, and it causes everyone around her to see it with those eyes. She's a beautiful character who shows people a beauty to their own world that they don't see. As she starts remembering who she was, she finds there's a darkness to her, but she gets a glimpse at living a different kind of life than she was ever meant for. She was meant to only be a warrior, and the heart of the story is that she gets to visit this world, almost as a newborn, and start a new life, have a father, have someone that she falls in love with, and it changes who she is. She doesn't have to go back to being what she was programmed to be. Getting that second chance at a life is really what makes her an incredible character, because she could easily just be a killing machine, and instead, by the end, she is living a life where she now knows what pain and sorrow and loss is. She has such great heart, which she never had before. So it shows how human nature can be. She is a human character, and we do point that out many times. She has an organic brain. She's not a machine, she's actually a person. Sometimes when you create a story about a cyborg or with similar futuristic elements, those types of movies can be very cold, and that's not Jim. It's like, 'Let's take this world and put a really great character story in it, one that's got really high stakes and where you really care for that character, and that character at the end of the day is very warm.' That's the power of Jim."

**LEFT:** Early (2005) concept art of Alita jumping down into the Underworld.
**RIGHT:** Concept art of Alita and the crashed URM warship.

# AFTERWORD

It is hard to believe that it has been almost twenty years since Guillermo del Toro brought the manga *Alita* to Lightstorm's attention. Despite the length of time it took for us to bring *Alita* to life on the big screen, Jim and I never stopped believing in the property. In fact, we think that many of the inherent themes of the story are even more relevant today than they were in 1999 when we first acquired the rights.

In the original manga series crafted by Yukito Kishiro, he created in Alita a character who comes into the story with no memory of who she is and who thinks of herself as just an insignificant girl. Kishiro takes her on a journey of self-discovery and personal empowerment, a story so strong and resonant that Jim identified *Alita* as a project he himself wanted to direct. Following a meeting in 2000 with Kishiro, Jim set out to write a script that would capture the scale and scope of the manga, while more importantly keeping the emotional and thematic qualities of the story.

It wasn't until 2005 that Jim, in collaboration with co-writer Laeta Kalogridis, finally had a script that he was ready to direct. At that same time however, technology had reached a point where we could start considering a movie that Jim had written a decade earlier… *Avatar*. Suddenly Jim had a dilemma… which movie to direct first? After close to a year of deliberation, Jim made the tough decision to direct *Avatar* first. With the success of *Avatar* and Jim's commitment to direct a number of sequels to the film, it become obvious that if we wanted to see *Alita* made within a reasonable time frame, we would need to find a director to partner with.

Over the course of the next several years, Jim and I had conversations with a number of potential directors, but could not find the right fit for this unique project. Then, in 2015, Robert Rodriguez visited Lightstorm for a social lunch with Jim. As the lunch was coming to a close, Robert asked Jim, "If you are going to be directing *Avatar* films for the foreseeable future, what happens to movies like *Alita: Battle Angel*?" A lightbulb went on in Jim's head and he asked Robert if he had fifteen minutes to look at something.

Jim showed Robert an "art reel" we had created in 2005 and Robert was hooked. Jim gave him a copy of the script, which was way too long at 186-pages, and told Robert that if he could shorten the script to a more appropriate shooting length, the movie was his to direct. Four months later, Robert presented a 128-page script. Jim and I were both astounded that, despite trimming so many pages, there was nothing in the core character or emotional story that we missed. We had found our partner with whom to bring *Alita* to life.

Under the watchful guidance of Jim and the directorial leadership of Robert, we combined the talents of key designers and concept artists already working for Lightstorm on the *Avatar* sequels with a team from Robert's Troublemaker Studios to design the characters and world of *Alita*. The strength of the script allowed us to attract an incredible cast, including four Oscar® nominees or winners. The entire cast, along with the artisans of Lightstorm, Troublemaker, and Weta, have brought unparalleled passion and dedication to the project.

Hopefully this book gave you a little insight into the exciting and rewarding experience we all had making *Alita*. We are all very proud of what was accomplished. I am thankful to Robert for the collaborative relationship we developed and enjoyed during the production, but more importantly, I am thankful for the friendship we formed.

—Jon Landau, *Producer*

**THIS IMAGE:** Concept art of Alita in her doll body befriending a stray dog.

# ACKNOWLEDGEMENTS

AUTHOR'S ACKNOWLEDGEMENTS: My deepest thanks to everyone who spoke with me for this book: Robert Rodriguez, Jon Landau, James Cameron, and (in alphabetical order) Richie Baneham, Dylan Cole, Fausto De Martini, A. Todd Holland, Richard Hollander, Joe Letteri, Steve Messing, John Park, Joe Pepe, Ben Procter, Nina Proctor, Eric Saindon, and Deborah Scott. Extra special thanks to Steve Joyner and Caylah Eddleblute for their incredible generosity not only with their interview time, but with their resources and enthusiasm. More thanks to Lightstorm's Joshua Izzo and Reymundo Perez, to my Titan Books editor extraordinaire Jo Boylett and to magnificent designer Tim Scrivens.

TITAN BOOKS would like to thank everyone who made time in their busy schedules for interviews and to supply material for this book, and all those whose work features in these pages. Special thanks to Robert Rodriguez for the Foreword and Jon Landau for the Afterword. Thanks also to all those who helped bring this book to fruition: Joshua Izzo, Reymundo Perez, and Billy Barnhart at Lightstorm Entertainment; Nicole Spiegel and Carol Roeder at 20th Century Fox; Natasha Turner and Dave Gougé at Weta Digital.

# ARTIST CREDITS

In alphabetical order: Jonathan Bach, Shane Baxley, Jonathan Berube, Michael Broom, Dawn Brown, Vitaly Bulgarov, Keith Christensen, James Chung, James Clyne, Dylan Cole, Fausto De Martini, Mark Goerner, Saiful Haque, Joseph Hiura, KNB EFX, Martin Laing, Ellen Lampl, Khang Le, Scott Lukowski, Stephan Martiniere, Steven Messing, Annis Naeem, Chris Olivia, John Park, Joseph C. Pepe, Joe Peterson, Ben Procter, Robert Simons, Tully Summers, Alex Toader, Weta Digital, Feng Zhu.

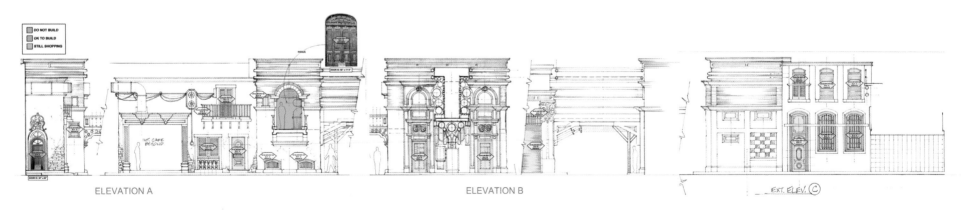

ELEVATION A          ELEVATION B          EXT. ELEV. C

**ABOVE:** Section of the blueprint for the Iron City slum district set.
**PREVIOUS SPREAD:** Final still of Hugo examining Alita's Berserker body hand.